ALSO BY STEPHANIE WINSTON

Getting Organized
The Organized Executive

ORGANIZED
FOR
SUCCESS

ORGANIZED
FOR
SUCCESS

• • •

Top Executives and CEOs
Reveal the Organizing Principles That
Helped Them Reach the Top

STEPHANIE WINSTON

CROWN
BUSINESS
NEW YORK

Published by Crown Business, New York, New York.
Member of the Crown Publishing Group, a division of Random House, Inc.
www.randomhouse.com

CROWN BUSINESS is a trademark and the Rising Sun colophon
is a registered trademark of Random House, Inc.

Printed in the United States of America

Design by Helene Berinsky

Library of Congress Cataloging-in-Publication Data

Winston, Stephanie.
    Organized for success : top executives and CEOs reveal the organizing
principles that helped them reach the top / Stephanie Winston.—1st ed.
        p. cm.
    1. Executives—Time management. I. Title.
HD69.T54W548 2004
658.4'093—dc22   2003025381

ISBN 1-4000-4759-5

10   9   8   7   6   5

First Edition

To the through-thick-and-thin five:
Dinah and Terry, Marnie, Norma and Sanford

Acknowledgments

It's hard to know where to start thanking the many people who have generously given their time, thoughts, and effort on behalf of *Organized for Success.*

First, of course, are the executives upon whose insights and extraordinary productivity this book rests. Many, many thanks to you for your time, your wisdom, and your genuine interest in sharing your experience. No one had ever asked you these questions before!

Many people very kindly opened executive doors for me, including: Marsha Albert, Julane Borth, Natalie Goldberg, Amy Hohn, Dinah and Fred Lovitch, Hadassah Markson, Karen Page, and Dee Soder.

One of the great privileges of preparing *Organized for Success* was the exhilarating opportunity to explore and develop ideas with numerous friends and colleagues. These people and their fine minds and wish to support me and *Organized for Success* contributed more than they know: Marsha Albert, Mark Chimsky, Barry Greisman, Lorie Greisman, Beth Lovitch, Dinah Lovitch, John Tepper Marlin, Karen Page, Terry Pickett, Tom Ranieri, Sanford Schmidt, and Carole Sinclair.

I want to especially thank three people at the heart of this enterprise: my editor, Annik LaFarge, whose unending interest and support, and whose enthusiasm for yet another round of batting around ideas, were exemplary; Nan Bauroth, writer/editor and friend, with great thanks for her major guidance and excellent judgment; and, superlatively, as always, the person who has guided me through more thickets than I can count, my colleague, cousin, and friend Marnie Winston-Macauley.

I would like to make special note of Michele Jaffe, who has prepared and typed this manuscript accurately and tirelessly through its many permutations. A bouquet of thanks. And thanks to Allison Futterman for all her help with admin and correspondence.

Thanks so much to my agent, Carole Sinclair, who launched *Organized for Success* and has shepherded it all along the way. Many thanks also to the Random House team, including my editor, Annik LaFarge; John Mahaney, executive editor for Crown Business; publicity manager Tara Gilbride; senior publicist Jason Gordon; copy editor David Wade Smith; and director of sales Doug Jones.

Contents

PART II
THE TOOLS OF SUCCESS
How Successful Executives Get Organized
Through To-Do Lists, Calendar/Planners,
the Telephone, and Technology

PART III
EXECUTIVE TIME AND
TASK MANAGEMENT

PART IV
USING CEO STRATEGIES
IN YOUR OWN DOMAIN

Introduction

Early in my career I felt that organization would destroy
my creativity. Whereas now, I feel the opposite.
Discipline is the concrete that allows you to be creative.

—VERNA GIBSON,
former president & CEO
The Limited/Victoria's Secret

For the past twenty years I have consulted with businesses both large
and small to develop techniques and strategies to help managers and
professionals establish organization in an overwhelming work environment. And I've studied the digitized technologies—computers,
PDAs, voice mail, e-mail—to develop ways for people to stay organized in the increasingly fast-paced and often chaotic workplace in
which we all find ourselves.

Yet, it's all just too much. I hear from managers every day that their
corporation is so lean and focused on productivity that they feel as if
they're now required to perform two, or even three, jobs. "There's just
so much of me to go around," people often say, revealing the increasing stress caused by workload demands.

One day, an interesting and surprising thought came to me. I suddenly realized that after all the years of consulting with the people who report to the top boss, no CEO who had risen up the ladder of a large organization had ever asked me to assist with their personal time-management and organizational practices.*

Yet, they have no more time during the day than you or I do. So I became curious. Surely every manager all the way up the line—including CEOs—faces the same fundamental organization and time-management challenges every day, and must deal with them at the warp speed at which most companies now work. So why is it that my services had never been tapped by up-the-ladder CEOs? How do they get so much accomplished in so little time? Is there something they know that we don't? Do they possess distinctive organizing skills and tactics not shared by the rest of us, and which, even in the midst of the digital revolution, have retained special potency? I suspected that many managers and professionals would be interested in finding out about the secrets of time and organizational mastery from executives who have achieved success. I decided to explore this question, and this book is the result.

At the outset I assumed that most senior executives would be functionally organized—otherwise they would not have made it to the top.

What I didn't anticipate, though, is that there is indeed a hidden organizing and time-management story among those who serve in the highest ranks of major organizations. In significant ways they *do* operate differently from the rest of us. And what is exciting is that

---

*Note that throughout this book, when I talk about the work styles of CEOs as a group, I'm referring to those who came up the ladder, rather than to entrepreneurs who run the companies they founded or co-founded. Unexpectedly, all up-through-the-ranks CEOs I am aware of share a startlingly similar organization and time-management style, whereas entrepreneurs are more individualistic. But all top executives offer many valuable insights.

their strategies are highly adaptable, in terms of both practical organizational disciplines and underlying mental disciplines—a decidedly strategic mindset rooted in a willingness to make decisions, and mastery of keeping their eyes on the prize.

But I'm also here to tell you another thing I discovered—something that even with my twenty years of experience in workplace organization I did not expect to find: CEOs who rise through major corporations appear to share, across industry lines, a kind of "effectiveness attitude" that incorporates six specific action-oriented organizational strategies.

No one has really looked at organization in this way. In this book I've attempted to distill and quantify these foundational organizing practices of CEOs and superexecutives into practical strategies that will enable you to adapt these executive insights to your own management style—thereby increasing your own potential for success. You want to make a contribution, you want to succeed, *and* you want to have a life.

This book is also addressed to the manager who wants the next job, who is interested in learning how successful executives used organization and time-management tools in unique ways to help launch themselves to the next level of success, significantly enlarging your ability to be powerful and effective within your own working environment.

My conclusions are based on a combination of interviews and free-ranging discussions with more than forty top executives from every business arena, as well as an extensive review of information from published sources.

The very good news for all of us is that these six fundamental executive practices and disciplines are readily adaptable to the day-to-day time-management programs of managers and executives at every level.

Six Action-Oriented Organizing Strategies

First: Three Facets of Executive Organization and Time Management

1: PERSONAL PRODUCTIVITY PROFILE

This facet of executive organization is about getting out from under and whiz-bang efficiency, solving problems like:

How do I get on top of e-mail overload?

Every time I start tackling my to-do list, a client calls and it gets put off.

It feels like I've got 900 interruptions every day and I've got to get my job done! What are some interruption-control strategies?

I go faster and faster every day, but never seem to get my priorities accomplished.

What this book will show you is that simple tactical choices—lining up the tools of productivity—can help you tremendously to accomplish goals. For example, in the chapter on e-mail, I highlight the tactics employed by one manager that reduced the number of e-mail reports he dealt with by 50 percent. Imagine how much more time that gave him to focus on the truly critical tasks at hand, and what a psychological lift he got from getting so much stuff out of his in-box and off his desk.

Tim Chamberlain, managing partner of Beverly Interiors in Dallas, explains on page 152 how color-coding client files helped him out of a time-management quicksand.

2: HOW EXECUTIVES TURN INTERRUPTIONS, MEETINGS, AND CASUAL CONTACTS INTO GOLD

With Facet 2, executive strategies begin to take a strange and unexpected turn.

I was genuinely astonished to find that most executives consider the meetings, interruptions, casual contacts, and frequent "gotta minute"s?

that pepper their day not as debits that subtract from their currency of time, but as assets—as opportunities that enrich their time.

Here's an example: One publishing professional I interviewed hand-carries materials downstairs to the production department several times a week, just for the opportunity to stop by and get a heads-up about a project from one person and an "Oh, I wanted you to see this" from another one.

Such strategies of collegiality—which I discovered are at the heart of the executives' organizational enterprise—can turn the casual contacts of the day into gold.

3: MANAGING INFLUENCE: THE ORGANIZING STRATEGIES THAT WILL PROPEL YOUR CAREER TO THE TOP

The third facet is a huge, myth-busting surprise. Over the course of my conversations with executives, a shadowy idea started to gain force.

In addition to the powerful strategies of Facet 1 and Facet 2, it began to seem to me that there was an x factor—a Facet 3: a set of exceptionally sophisticated organizing skills that informs the day-to-day organizational strategies of top executives.

I call this obscure aspect of organizing "managing influence."

At its core, managing influence is a process of supercharging each casual encounter—just the normal drop-bys, queries, etc.—with a small extra charge or punch.

Over the course of days, weeks, months, and years, the accumulated power of these charged contacts will help propel a manager, assuming all other business skills being equal, toward the top. The concept is developed in chapter 14, Using CEO Strategies in Your Own Domain.

Second: Three Powerful Executive Tools

The desire of senior managers and executives to produce maximum results from their daily activities stems from another set of characteristics—arteries, if you will, that thread through all their activities.

1. The decision-making imperative. Perhaps the key attribute of people at the top is that they are decisive. But there's a kicker: Generally speaking, the big-picture decisions are reached through a long process of consensus building that is not at all like the Lone Ranger image that most imagine.

The decision-making imperative is primarily expressed day-to-day in Facet 1; no papers are left on the desk or e-mails in the in-box because those decisions are made as-they-go in real time.

The heart of this decision-making process is described in Chapter 1, Ruthless Paperwork: How Executives Get to a Clean Desk.

2. Focus, focus, focus. Surprise: The accepted wisdom that the ultimate test of management smarts is the ability to multitask is not supported by my observations. Those who rise to the top in Fortune 500 corporations hardly multitask at all.

Rather, inherent in the executive style is the ability to keep a laser focus—albeit for only minutes or even seconds at a time—on whatever is in front of them until the matter is completed. They have the distinct ability to avoid becoming distracted. Bill Gates, for example, won't even read while he is on his exercise bike.

3. Keep your eyes on the prize. Senior executives are characterized by an ability to always keep in mind a few dominant priorities around which they organize their day-to-day activities.

There are two types of priorities in the executive's lexicon: the important tasks that preoccupy him or her every day, week, and year; but also, equally important, priority themes. For example, Jack Welch's whole career has been informed by a personal theme: cultivate the best people.

How master executives cope with establishing a productive balance between the daily pressures and tasks and their broader priorities is a constant thread that weaves through *Organized for Success*.

Finding Your Own Time-Management Path

One of the great skills shared by top executives is their ability to enable others. But since they can't speak to you directly, they have chosen this book as the tool that will enable you to benefit from their tools, secrets, and time-management strategies.

One of the key organizing lessons is that one size does not fit all. In this book you'll learn how successful executives figured out what tools, tactics, and strategies worked best for them, and then built upon that knowledge to develop their personal pathway to effectiveness.

Take one simple idea: using your prime time wisely. Several executives spoke of soaring productivity once they had identified their personal peak time—and the clever stratagems they found to carve out a power hour for themselves to accomplish their priorities and hardest tasks.

The moral, in the phrase of Kerr-McGee CEO Luke Corbett, is be yourself. Take Mr. Corbett's message to heart to design your own organizing profile. Lead with your strong suit, and compensate for what is not strongest to create a complete executive package.

From the day top executives begin work at the entry level, they see their office as a means of fulfilling their own potential and that of the company to the greatest degree possible. And whether you're aiming for the top, or simply wish to enhance your productivity in the position you're occupying now, you can use the information here to enhance your productivity and *multiply* time.

By adapting executive tactics, you can operate as a CEO in your own domain.

To start things off, here's one more secret I picked up from CEOs that you can start using today, no matter what your field of endeavor. I call it the "capture book."

In essence, the capture book is a small notebook that many top executives carry with them or keep on their desks to jot down phone numbers, queries, thoughts, ideas, sources, and so on, as they occur. For other executives, it may be more of an "ideas" book.

Richard Branson, founder of the Virgin Companies, has collected more than 100 of these notebooks over the years and says he won't ever throw them away. He's learned that these spontaneous records of brainstorms, concerns, potential resources, and thoughts are an invaluable asset.

How to Use This Book to Develop Your Personal Executive Productivity Profile

Organized for Success is your book, so use it the way that most benefits you. My suggestion is to first read through the entire book, using the table of contents as a roadmap. Place a check mark beside those chapters that speak to or address a personal priority or concern.

Then adapt and adopt the ideas that will have the greatest impact on your personal productivity by starting with the first chapter you've checked. For instance, if managing e-mail is a huge problem for you, then start there. And be sure to undertake the exercises I suggest to implement strategies that make sense to you. By using these CEO strategies in your own domain, you will begin to incorporate and actually change your attitudes and effectiveness in the realm of organization and time management.

To kick-start your thinking, here is a summary of the questions I have tried to answer about the hidden organization and time-management life of successful CEOs:

How do they get it all done every day?

How do they keep from being overwhelmed by interruptions?

Why are their desks and e-mail in-boxes almost always clear?

How do they find what they need, when they need it?

How do they keep meetings on track and productive?

What are their strategies to accomplish priorities and not get distracted from the most important things?

How do they get more accomplished in less time?

· What are their strategies of effective delegation?

Nine Organization and Time-Management Strategies of Highly Successful Executives

The distinctive characteristics of CEOs, combined with their practical tactics, can be summarized in nine strategies that form an executive profile in productivity you can mold to your own needs.

➤ FUNDAMENTALS OF ORGANIZATION AND TIME MANAGEMENT

1. *Plow through papers and deskwork quickly.* Achieve a clear desk. A habit of decision-making combined with an attitude of commitment will get you to that clear desk.

2. *Conquer the e-mail clutter.* Employ a three-point e-mail program to bring the e-mail tiger under control: shrink the number of e-mails you receive in the first place; prioritize; and apply a host of e-mail efficiency methods.

3. *Follow through tenaciously—don't let anything fall through the cracks.* Combine simple follow-through tools with an attitude—almost a relentless compulsion—to see something through to completion. Call it a bulldog attitude—don't let go until it's done.

4. *Enhance effectiveness through technology.* Phones, PDAs, laptops, virtual meetings—take advantage of every available technology to upgrade your effectiveness.

HOW SUCCESSFUL EXECUTIVES "DO" TIME MANAGEMENT

5. *Manage time and tasks.* Accomplish tasks in an efficient and timely way. Surprise: "Multitasking" is out; "spotlighting" is in.

6. *Embrace the timesavers and avoid the timewasters.* Useful and proven timesaving executive tips.

STRIVING FOR THE TOP: KEY EXECUTIVE SKILLS

7. *Focus on the right things—and achieve superlative results.* Being a senior executive involves effectively managing multiple priorities.

8. *Transform interruptions and distractions from an annoyance into a career-building asset.* Successful executives turn one key time-management rule upside down: rather than closing the door to interruptions, they extract genuine value from them.

9. *Multiply your productivity through effective delegation.* The art of senior executives, supported by all the strategies described, is to freely delegate both tasks and responsibilities, and then to empower those staffers to be as effective as possible.

What would it take to make your day look a little bit more like the day of a top executive? First, gradually integrate the strategies themselves. You may not have an executive's staff, but you can adopt their habits. Find your own style. Develop a plan and make it your own.

How do people go about replacing old attitudes with new ones? How do people become disciplined? Truly, it can be done. And in this book I'll help you organize and retool yourself so you can take the lessons of these corporate leaders and use them to lock in supercharged productivity.

These CEOs and other top executives have a great deal to tell you. I hope you will consider investing in your future by thinking of *Organized for Success* as your personal roadmap to help you be as organized—and as successful in your work—as you can be.

I'm often reminded of something that Charles R. Schwab wrote in his first book, *Charles Schwab's Guide to Financial Independence,* about the importance of investing. "Read this book," he said. "Try out the suggestions. But please do *something,* because the biggest risk in investing is doing nothing." The same is true of organization. As soon as you start, you're two steps closer to your hopes of productivity and professional security. I wish you the best as you begin.

PART I

THE FUNDAMENTAL TOOLS OF ORGANIZATION AND TIME MANAGEMENT

• • •

1

Ruthless Paperwork

• • •

HOW EXECUTIVES GET TO A CLEAN DESK

Mark Green, a New York City political figure, spoke for many of us when he said, "My desk looks like Pompeii after the eruption. These [chief executive] guys run [enormous] enterprises and they always have a clean desk. Why?"

Green was on the money. Even in this digital age, there are plenty of overloaded desks out there. But those desks on overload are *not* the desks of senior executives.

Take a look at the desk of Akira Chiba, president of Pokémon USA. On its glass expanse sit a computer, desk accessories, memorabilia, and a small stack of papers representing current projects that Mr. Chiba is following. That's all—except for an oversized Pokémon doll perched nearby.

Mr. Chiba's desk at least has a lived-in look. Other executives' desks are as vacant as the lunar surface.

If you've ever been in the office of a corporate CEO, you've probably observed this clean-desk phenomenon, and wondered how he or she does it. Is there some secret paper-management process (we'll discuss e-mail separately) they practice, that you don't, to achieve their spartan deskscape?

When I began to explore the organization and time-management practices of top executives, I took it for granted that they were adept at managing the paper flow, simply because I'd seen too many promising careers stunted by a failure to process paperwork and e-mail in a timely way. So I figured they'd found ways to end-run that traditional office-organization trap. That assumption was correct, but with an unexpected twist: CEOs are absolutely *ruthless* when dealing with paperwork.

I actually clocked how long it takes for an average document, once having hit the in-box of a chief executive, to turn around again.

What's your guess? A week? Two days? Try ten minutes—literally.

Top executives just can't stand to let things linger. One executive referred to his insistence on getting paper off his desk and out again as "pathological." I don't know. Sounds pretty good to me.

So pronounced is this senior executive tendency to clear their desks, one way or another, down to the shine, that I nominate this as "Organizing Law No. 1":

ORGANIZING LAW NO. 1:
Relentlessly process all papers and e-mails,
personally or through an assistant.

TRAF: The Four Decisions to a Clean Desk

What's the how-to on getting to those clean desks? I'll bet when you envision Fortune 500 executives sitting at their desks pushing through papers and e-mail, you imagine an entire suite of administrative assistants taking charge of the process. Once you reach that corporate pinnacle, such a scenario is not unreasonable. But here's the real kicker: These leaders practiced ruthless paperwork habits long before they reached the top rung! When the executive was a brand manager or a junior financial analyst, his or her desk would have looked exactly the same as it does today.

The big news here is that the real heart and soul of having a clean desk is not a genetic trait or innate genius or fleets of assistants. It's simply based on a portfolio of four decisions that executives make in dealing with every single document that comes their way.

Everyone knows Alan Lakein's classic mantra, "Handle each piece of paper only once." Good advice, if sometimes unrealistic. But handle *how*? What are your options? Happily, I've discovered there are only four things you can do with a piece of paper—four decisions:

Toss it

Refer it (i.e., pass it along or discuss it with someone else)

Act on it personally

File it

I call this the TRAF system. (TRAF is discussed in detail in my earlier book *The Organized Executive*.)

TRAF is a powerful decision-making tool, because it provides a fixed template to test any action you contemplate with regard to a piece of paper.

For example, you've received a brochure for an industry conference six months hence. Here's how to TRAF it:

Toss—No interest? Out.

Refer—Of interest to Rick? Pop it over.

Act—Wish to go? Send in the form. Too early to decide? "Resurface" the brochure in a month or two (see page 22), and decide then.

File—Maybe you collect sample brochures? File it.

Overcoming Obstacles to TRAF

Have you ever looked at stacks of paper or a list of unread e-mails, and it all blurred together? Of course it's intimidating! Of course it's overwhelming! Of course you'd rather do almost anything than work through those piles.

Below are two strategic techniques executives use that will enable you to plow speedily through that paper and arrive at that coveted clean desk.

"Mosaic" focus. Productivity guru David Allen has pointed out that it's hard to be productive when you have 265 things gnawing at you. Allen says, in *Work Smarter Not Harder: Roadmap to Success* (Fast Company, 1998), "Productivity is about completion. [It's about] identifying the 'incompletions' in your life, and taking the next step." As I watched executives process their paperwork and e-mail, I noticed the real reason it's impossible for them to suffer desk buildup: they maintain an intense concentration on each individual item until it has been addressed—no matter what the subject.

The focused gaze might last no more than ten seconds. But in that ten seconds the executive has made the TRAF decision and physically completed the action, if only to toss the item or put it into a folder to discuss later with a colleague, or scribbled a note and put it in the outbox.

They almost all share a kind of bulldog grip that simply won't loosen until the document in their field of vision has been dealt with. They concentrate on each item as you might concentrate on a small piece of mosaic tile—handling it by putting each piece, one by one, into its proper place.

If focusing on the individual document—which could be a yellow sticky on your computer or a scribbled phone number on the back of an envelope—doesn't come naturally to you, here's an exercise that will help "mosaic focus" become a natural, instinctive process:

1. Count out ten or fewer documents on your desk. On a legal pad, put a big numeral "1." Then TRAF—Toss, Refer, Act, or File—the first document only. Don't forget to mark the item for pop-up in your calendar or computer when you need to revisit the outcome. When you've taken action, check off the "1"! That feels good.

2. Next, write the numeral "2" and TRAF again. Keep going for no more than ten items, and then break.

3. Over the course of the day, try to complete that day's incoming materials.

I'll wager that within three to four weeks after systematically focusing on the TRAF process day after day, "mosaic focus" will seem natural and intuitive.

Catch up on backlog. Once you've gotten the rhythm of daily TRAFing, TRAF a package of items two or three times a week from your backlog stack. You'll be amazed at how rapidly the backlog will evaporate.

Correction, not perfection. What about the possibility of making the wrong TRAF decision? It happens, surely. But the consensus among top executives is that almost any mistake can be corrected. So look at every one of your small TRAF decisions as an opportunity for a later correction in course, rather than as a "mistake" waiting to be engraved on your forehead.

What CEOs demonstrate is that making a decision is much more important than always being right. Making many small decisions will strengthen your decision-making muscle every day, and enable you to handle paperwork like a CEO in your own domain.

In fact, so central is this decision-oriented mindset to the effective functioning of senior executives that I call it "Organizing Law No. 2."

ORGANIZING LAW NO. 2:
Make decisions, even if
they need to be revised later.

Two more paper-mastery recommendations:

1. *Set two or three "dedicated" times during the day to process papers and e-mail.* Most executives arrive at 7:00 or 7:30 a.m. to clear the decks. Try a half hour first thing, or just after your coffee break. Slot two other fifteen-minute TRAF sessions later in the day to relieve paperwork and e-mail pressure.

2. *What about urgent e-mails during the day?* Set your filters to "alarm" you for e-mails from your boss, key clients, and other important people.

Following Up and Following Through:
A Fundamental Time Multiplier

Failure to meet deadlines, honor commitments, monitor staff, return calls, and keep track of long-term projects is the most underrated cause of chaos and failure in business life. Strong words, but true. Here are three commonplace examples of consequences that often occur when a strong hand is not maintained on following up and following through:

- One creative director replied to an e-mail requesting a look at new website graphics by saying, "I'll get back to you next Wednesday." He forgot, and had to be prompted again—twice. Now his colleagues say about him, "Sure, he's a nice guy, and talented, but you just can't count on him."
- A marketer supporting a campaign to open a new market among physicians had called an associate to get a line on "who's who" in the medical association world. The source was on vacation, so

the marketer forgot to follow up—until her boss, who hadn't forgotten, stormed in demanding the information.

- A pharmaceutical company attorney who was responsible for handling a sensitive discrimination claim did not follow up appropriately in filing documents, etc.—to the degree that, although he is a skilled lawyer, he was removed from the matter. If he should drop the ball comparably again, his job will go into play.

So important are the benefits of strong, consistent follow-up that this is Organizing Law No. 3.

ORGANIZING LAW NO. 3:
Foolproof follow-up is a linchpin of organization.

On a day-to-day basis, consistent, automatic follow-up can deflect a lot of the firefighting that can push your day off course. But the mistake so many people make is to trust their memory. When you say, "I'll call you next Thursday," who's going to remember that? Not you, not me, not anyone of my acquaintance.

The first step in restoring reliable follow-up to its place of honor as one of the fundamental tools of organization and time management is to drop "remembering" from your vocabulary.

In order to banish the phrase "I forgot," systematically integrate the simple follow-up techniques that follow. But don't see following up as just another burden. On the contrary, once you've entered your prompt into your planner, tickler, or PDA, it's off your mind—not racketing around in your head with all the many other things you've got to remember. A hallmark of an effective follow-up system is that memory truly drops out of the equation.

Since specific executive follow-up tactics are enumerated throughout this book, here's a summarized roundup of tactics and strategies.

Prompts

A "prompt" is a reminder that pops up on your computer or in your paper planner at the appropriate time. *Benefit:* You can simply drop the matter from your mind until it resurfaces.

Here are some prompting tactics:

PLANNER/"PENDING FILE" METHOD

Tools: Your planner (whether paper, computer, or PDA) and a dedicated paper "pending" file folder, or a computer file, to hold any documents connected with the reminder. Perhaps you might use a green or red file folder to distinguish it from your other files.

Method: A client asks you to call next Thursday to review an important cover letter over the phone. You mark a very brief reminder in your planner for Thursday, "Call Joe re letter." (I usually also enter the phone number so I don't have to look it up again.)

Drop a copy of the letter into your pending file.

End of story until the reminder pops up in your planner.

Since no one can always act on every follow-up at the appointed time—for example, an unexpected meeting might prevent you from making a call you had scheduled for Wednesday—make sure that follow-ups do not get passed by. Daily, if possible, but at least weekly, reenter any uncompleted follow-ups into another day, crossing them off at their original location.

When a follow-up comes up on the fly—say someone asks you at a luncheon to get back to them next week—it might be too cumbersome to pull out your calendar or PDA at that moment.

Tip: Follow the lead of Bill Bratton, America's "top cop," and Arthur Levitt, head of the SEC in the Clinton administration and Wall Street insider, by always carrying an index card or sticky pad in your pocket, when you're out and about, to capture these on-the-fly notes. Then, as one of your end-of-the-day rituals, enter them as prompts into your planner, or take the suggestion of executive James

M. Morris, Chairman & CEO of Signator (an affiliated John Hancock company): If it's not convenient for him to write down a reminder or follow-up, he'll call the reminder in to his own voice-mail box.

THE "TICKLER FILE"

The "tickler" is a tried-and-true method of keeping track of promises you need to keep and items you need to track.

Here is a description of the classic tickler file, with an index-card variation:

Prepare, or ask your assistant to prepare, thirty-one file folders labeled 1–31. Also prepare an additional set of folders, labeled January through December.

Okay, you've promised to get back to an associate regarding an outstanding project next Thursday—which is the seventeenth of the month.

Simply drop a reminder note into the folder labeled "17," along with any relevant materials—no muss, no fuss.

On the seventeenth, pull out the "17" folder, and TRAF all the follow-ups and materials in that day folder. Tomorrow you'll TRAF the "18" folder, and so on around the month.

Longer-term follow-ups: Say it's January and you've got a follow-up pegged for March. Drop the materials into the "March" folder, and at the beginning of March, distribute its contents into specific days. At the beginning of each month, distribute that month's accumulation similarly.

Great tickler advantage: The tickler file is a great place to store any materials relative to a specific event, or travel documents. For example, got a meeting on the sixteenth? Drop the agenda into the "16" folder. Or if you want to retrieve the agenda the day before, drop it into "15." Handle travel tickets and other documents similarly.

The index-card tickler. Some people prefer to write each follow-up item or task on its own index card. Then the cards are filed in a file box, using the same numbered dividers as with a tickler file. With this system, you would collect backup materials in a single "pending file" as described earlier in connection with the calendar prompt.

In his book *The Present* (Doubleday, 2003), Spencer Johnson, author of *Who Moved My Cheese?*, makes the point that completion of one project or task—taking care of the loose end—no matter how inconsequential in itself, seems to "build energy and confidence to succeed in the next task." There is no doubt in my mind that the loose ends will kill you. Even if they are not particularly important in themselves, they will catch you in a sticky trap that can materially hobble your productivity and effectiveness over the long term.

THE VIEW FROM THE EXECUTIVE DESK

Most chief executives' offices in large corporations tend to be about the size of basketball courts. In New York they may have a drop-dead view of Central Park or the Statue of Liberty; in San Francisco, of the Golden Gate Bridge; in St. Louis, of the Arch. In addition to an enormous desk, most executives' offices feature a sitting-room area with a couch and soft chairs, and a small conference table for meetings with direct reports and other small groups.

But there's an intriguing split in the approach to decor between rung-by-rung executives and entrepreneurial chief executives, in that the offices of entrepreneurs are apt to express that individual's personal taste and temperament.

For example, the office of Martin Edelston, founder of Boardroom, Inc., publishers of Bottom Line/Personal and some forty other business and personal newsletters, is a wonderful expression of his vivid, imaginative personality. Edelston's office is decorated exuberantly, with lots of bright artwork. At one time the main feature of his office was a working jukebox.

The New York office of Arthur Levitt, before he became head of the SEC, featured wonderful enlarged photographs of wild animals, which he had taken while on safari in Africa.

The offices of up-the-ladder executives, on the other hand, show no such personal idiosyncrasies. Large, handsome, and austere, their offices are seats of power, but of an anonymous sort. The offices look as if the executives all bought their interiors at the same CEO store.

Ask the Executives

Here are some FAQs people often ask senior executives about their organization habits:

How do you handle paperwork when you're away for several days?

Marcia Zerivitz, executive director of the Jewish Museum of Florida, says, "My assistant is very good at that. Mail is sorted into three categories. One is third class—advertising mail, that sort of thing. And then the other two main categories—anything related to finances and correspondence she knows I have to look at—she'll put into their own folders. When I get back, I look through the two main categories immediately—usually within the first hour of my return. The third-class mail I'll take home and glance at over the weekend. Most will go in the trash."

If you don't have an assistant to sort things out for you, try these two alternatives:

1. Prevent buildup by asking a colleague or the department assistant to sweep up all incoming materials and express them to you

at least every other day, so that you can deal with them while you are away.

2. If handling as you go isn't practical, then create an island of dedicated time on your return—early, late, or on the weekend—to catch up. Otherwise you will feel inundated.

Can you suggest some tactics for effective communication with an assistant?

Some executives handle incoming papers in large part themselves, while others, as they progress in their careers, turn over "vetting" authority to an assistant.

John Curley told me an amusing story of how the quantity of mail that hit his desk shrank sharply down to two or three pieces when he first took over the chairmanship of Gannett in 1989 from his flamboyant predecessor, Allen Neuharth.

When he asked his secretary—who had been Neuharth's secretary—where all the mail was, she explained that Neuharth had instructed her to severely prescreen his mail, and she had just continued to do so.

Curley asked her to "open things up," and again started receiving the much broader range of materials he preferred.

Here are some more tips:

- One executive's favorite desk-clearing tactic—a strategy so effective I call it the "magic technique"—is to sit down every morning with his assistant for about twenty minutes (no interruptions or calls allowed). After collecting all the incoming paperwork and printing out important e-mails, his executive assistant sits across from him and they go through each item individually.

  The executive gives her instructions for each item—for example, "Call a meeting with Art for Tuesday to discuss the Dallas situation." After going through the pile, the executive is usually left with no more than two or three items that he has to process on his own.

- A school board executive reports that she and her assistant pass a single bright red folder back and forth to each other during the day. The assistant will put papers to sign and notes for the executive to review into it. The executive places into the folder tasks that she wants her assistant to do. They have a mutual commitment that by the end of the day everything in the red folder has been addressed, and the folder is empty and ready to start off the next day.

We've got too many useless reports washing around. How can we get them under control?

When John Sutton became CEO of Precision Machine Company in Seattle, he noticed that many subordinates ignored the thick computer reports they received. They only saved the paper clips, throwing the actual reports into the wastebasket. So Sutton instituted three ingenious methods to free his organization from needless reports:

1. He killed reports that people didn't read, killing each report in sequence. Unless people protested, he didn't resurrect them.

2. He held annual "kill report" meetings. At least three reports had to be eliminated at these meetings. Asking everyone which reports they used, he killed any report that didn't directly lead to action.

3. He put reports on the intranet and counted the visitors. He killed any reports that drew few or no visits.

The great theater impresario David Belasco said that if you couldn't write your idea down on the back of a business card, you hadn't thought it through.

Other fans of slimmed-down reports included Winston Churchill, Ronald Reagan, and the founder of Hallmark Cards, Joyce Hall, who all insisted that memos be summarized on one page.

What are some specific techniques used by famous executives?

Jack Welch got the facts fast. He wasted no time trying to "wing it" when he wasn't familiar with the jargon or complexities of a business. Instead he had someone break them down into terms he could understand. As he says in his book *Jack: Straight from the Gut,* "In [my] early days, I didn't understand the intricacies of finance. I had the staff prepare a book that translated all the jargon into layman's terms. I called it 'finance for little folks,' but it was just what I needed. I studied like I was back in grad school so I could be conversant with the people in the business."

You can adapt Jack Welch's "little folks" technique with this trick I learned from a journalist friend: get the basics by reading a book intended for ten- to fourteen-year-olds.

My friend was once assigned a story about the fashion industry about which she knew nothing. So she picked up one of those career guides titled something like "So You Want to Be in Fashion?" It was basic, clear, and complete. Armed with the basic facts, she had the context she needed for her story.

The legendary John D. Rockefeller, who amassed an oil empire, was an expert at TRAF, though he didn't call it that. His private secretary, George D. Rogers, said the tycoon adhered to this routine to deal with the daily paperwork deluge:

Unfinished business, letters, telegrams, memos, and the like were placed in a pile on the right-hand side of Rockefeller's desk. He would take up the first paper that came to hand, issue his instructions, or turn it over to someone else to handle. When the matter was addressed, the papers were filed.

If the paper could not be immediately attended to, Rockefeller turned it facedown on the left-hand side of his desk. When the pile on the right was all taken care of, he would turn the left pile faceup and move it to the right side to be dealt with again the following day. In later days, nothing was left on his desk but the deskpad, a blotter, pen, ink, and pencils.

ORGANIZED CLUTTER AS A FAIL-SAFE PAPERWORK SYSTEM

An experience with a colleague taught me that there's "bad" clutter, and then there's "organized" clutter.

I had been working on a project by phone, fax, and e-mail with a marketing executive in Philadelphia I'd never met. She had always seemed very well organized, so I was surprised, at our first meeting, to find stacks and stacks of papers on and around her desk. It looked a towering mess.

Curious, I asked her about it. She laughed and said, "I'm a visual person. If I don't see it, it doesn't exist. But I have a system!" She explained that at the center of her desk was her planner. Around the planner in a semicircle were the "hot" items she was actively working on (our project materials were right there). Lining the rim of her desk were staff projects and items she was monitoring. And, finally, on the floor around her desk lay current project files.

Her method for keeping this mass of material under control was simplicity itself. Every Friday she went from pile to pile—actually touching each stack so as not to "lose her place"—checking what tasks and follow-ups would be relevant in the coming week.

She listed all outstanding items on blue paper she used only for this purpose—and put that list in the center of her desk.

First thing Monday morning she got to work.

Her system worked!

2

Conquering E-mail Clutter

• • •

When I ask senior executives how they use e-mail, their comments are marked by a curious and unexpected hesitancy—wariness, even. A surprising number of them—including Leonard A. Lauder, chairman of Estée Lauder; Teodoro Benavides, city manager of Dallas; and Akira Chiba, president of Pokémon USA—expressed the concern that, when used incorrectly, e-mail could actually impede rather than foster communication. William G. Dugan, a publisher at Briefings Communications, a newsletter publisher in Alexandria, Virginia, summed it up succinctly: "E-mail is an indispensable task tool. But to allow it to encroach on your human interaction with people is a very damaging attitude. E-mail tends to be a separating influence rather than a unifying one. You, as a leader, have a responsibility to create an environment of teamwork."

These concerns, however, represent only half of the e-mail paradox. There is no doubt that managerial work in the last decade has been totally transformed by rapid e-mail communication—now made even more instantaneous with the widespread adoption of instant messaging. No executive could imagine life without it.

The other half of the e-mail dilemma is "death by drowning." With many organizations now relying on e-mail as the dominant method of communication, the nonexistent gap between an idea in your head and tapping out an e-mail, along with copies to ten of your colleagues, has created an e-mail tidal wave. Under 100 e-mails a day is considered a modest quantity; up to 200 has become commonplace in certain industries; and 300 or more is not unheard of. So, to deal with both aspects of e-mail culture, I've divided this chapter into two sections:

E-mail efficiency—what and how. This section begins with a fascinating case history of how one executive, Idit Harel, founder and CEO of MaMaMedia, Inc., an interactive website for children, created a productive e-mail culture at her company. Then I'll share numerous successful e-mail strategies you can use, from a wide range of executives and managers.

An exploration of executive unease about the Law of Unintended Consequences as e-mail has come to play a predominant role in workplace communication.

Reducing the E-mail Glut, and Other Executive Strategies and Tactics

CEOs TRAF e-mails as they do paper, with a digital twist:

Toss = Delete
Refer = Forward
Act = Act
File = Archive

But then things start to get complicated. Here is a wonderful case history of how one executive wrestled e-mail to the ground at her company:

At the Desk of Idit Harel: Creating a Productive E-mail Culture

Idit Harel is an Israeli-born computer whiz with a PhD from MIT. We met in the pleasant, brick-walled offices of her company, MaMaMedia, Inc., in New York's SoHo district, where she and her employees operate in an open-plan environment. But as in many offices, there was so much internal e-mailing that people were getting inundated. To help her staff get their heads above water, Ms. Harel thought through an e-mail management strategy for herself and her team.

In her view, her job is to shape e-mail to her company's own purposes. Ms. Harel's three keys to e-mail management are (1) shaping the e-mail; (2) prompt acknowledgment and convenient response; and (3) establishing an internal e-mail courtesy code through a "culture of consultation."

Shaping the e-mail. Says Ms. Harel, "You need to establish a common vocabulary, so you'll understand an e-mail's meaning—its urgency, how thoroughly you need to study it, versus just being informed."

The main tool is to ensure that the e-mail has a specific subject line. To compose an effective subject line, use the following criteria:

- Use the subject line to convey the nature of the e-mail: "Action required," "FYI," "Meeting update," etc.
- When possible, put the entire message in the subject line so the e-mail doesn't need to be opened. For example, "Meeting at 3:00 p.m. Thursday is on." "I'll be in Chicago on Th & Fr." "Need by the 28th."

Ms. Harel notes her preference for a taxonomy of subject lines—the little "post-y" things like "touching base" or "urgent" or "FYI."

"People need to learn to write an e-mail so that it communicates.

Focus the reader's attention on the highlights so they don't have to wade through: 'Please read paragraph 2.' It's like highlighting on paper. Or offer a summary."

The two-phrase response: first acknowledge, then reply.

"I have many days with 200 e-mails a day, yet I rarely feel overwhelmed," she told me.

"Why not?" I asked. "Everybody else does."

She attributes her comfort level to her "first acknowledge, then respond" approach. "I make a point," says Ms. Harel, "of acknowledging every e-mail as soon as I can. But the misconception is that you have to actually reply fast. I prioritize e-mails based on the day's events, using a two-phase approach."

Ms. Harel first "manages expectations" by acknowledging e-mails almost instantly, giving her breathing space to reply at a more convenient time. She uses these acknowledgment lines:

"I just received it. I probably won't get back to you till next week."

"I got it, read it, and will read it again—and I'm going to respond next week."

"Got it, read it, and here's my quick response. Expect a longer one next week."

Ms. Harel emphasizes that you must arrange follow-up prompts so you will reply when you said you would, or your credibility is shot.

Then she returns e-mails, within whatever time frame she has established, opportunistically—in a taxi, late at night, walking to an appointment, during a train commute, in the elevator, or taking a coffee break at Starbucks. She keeps up-to-date all day, distributing her responses over time, in intervals that are convenient to her, which greatly relieves the sense of pressure so many people experience.

Establishing a "culture of consultation." Ms. Harel has established a process that is, in my experience, unique: regular company strategy meetings specifically focused on keeping e-mails productive. They discuss issues such as these:

- *Whom do you send the e-mail to?* "Who should be in the recipient line, or cc'd, or bcc'd, to achieve maximum efficiency?" For instance, she asks that staff copy her assistant on meeting announcements, so if she doesn't respond, her assistant can follow up.

- *Establish clearer dissemination routines.* Ms. Harel's team regularly revisits criteria for forwarding e-mails. For instance, it's okay to be taken off the distribution list for this project because "it's *not* important for you to see the process. When we have the outcome, we'll let you know."

- *Limit your individual mailing list.* To avoid having her staff bombarded by personal messages like "My cat needs a new home. I'm allergic," Ms. Harel developed a "push-pull" concept, in which it's okay to send individual messages to your ten closest colleagues ("push" the message), but not to fifty or a hundred people. Instead, post your message on a company "digital bulletin board" that people can "pull" at lunchtime or their convenience.

- *Ask!* Staff now asks, "Do you want to be bcc'd on this?" Someone might be blind-copied about a project in an ongoing negotiation, and then read it a week later when the project is concluded to keep up to speed. This keeps them in the loop without pressure.

Such consistent consultation reflects an attitude of continuous improvement. In Ms. Harel's words, "Keep the things that work, transform the things that don't."

THE SIX-POINT E-MAIL COURTESY PROGRAM

E-mail seems to have shortened the time gap between a thought and its dissemination. People who would never dream of calling a colleague five or six times a day to chat, don't hesitate to fire off an e-mail at a random thought, along with ten copies to other colleagues.

STOP!

Everyone is just worn down by the e-mail onslaught. As a kindness to your colleagues, consider these six points each time you impulsively begin to send an e-mail:

1. Can this information be held for a meeting or another convenient time?
2. Can it be summarized?
3. Can it be subsumed into a broader status report?
4. Is there a real "need to know"?
5. How many people *really* want or need to be copied?
6. **Important:** If your e-mail is part of a long series, it would be very, very considerate to begin with a two- or three-sentence recap so people don't have to go back and read the old e-mails trailing your message.

More Great Executive E-mail Strategies

REDUCING E-MAILS

Drowning in e-mail? Here are several executives' tactics to reduce the flood.

Nader Karimi, vice-president of Emerging Technology for Twentieth Century Fox, rebelled against the 150 daily e-mails that consumed hours of his day. He simply asked his staff to cut back sharply on the "cc" and "FYI" e-mails they sent him, which slimmed his e-mail in-box by more than 50 percent! From the standpoint of senders, this requires some thought: Ask yourself if an e-mail requires any definite action by the recipient, or if the information could be disseminated in a more pertinent form.

Wayne Forehand, vice-president of Energy Distribution, Florida Power Corp., uses another method to cut e-mails: he returns unnecessary messages from his staffers with a note saying, "I don't need this." He tells them, "Don't be hurt, I'm trying to reduce my e-mails. Keep sending, but get a feel for the kind of material I don't need to see." Criterion: "If you had to put this in an envelope, stamp and mail it, would you send this to me?" Forehand is careful in his return note that his tone is cordial, recognizing how harsh e-mails can seem to the recipient when the sender didn't mean to offend.

Message: Reread everything for tone before you send it.

Garry Hart, founder and CEO of Fathom Pictures, a producer of computer games, says in David Allen's book *Work Smarter Not Harder:* "I maintain a private e-mail account to which fewer than a dozen people have the address. Messages sent to the company's e-mail address are screened by my assistant."

STAYING IN THE LOOP EFFICIENTLY

Nader Karimi insists that status reports be streamlined into bulleted, one-page memos. "I trust my management team to handle a lot of issues and filter that information to me through status reports."

Idit Harel stays up-to-date with a weekly e-mail "snapshot" of events from her marketing, sales, customer relations, and design departments. She has the option of requesting more background material if she wishes more detail.

GREAT STRATEGIES WHEN YOU HAVE A FULL-TIME ASSISTANT

To release evenings spent handling the 150-plus e-mails he got each day, Scott Baxter of JPMorganChase asked his assistant, Pat, to review his daily e-mails. She alerts him to important e-mails, and prints out the non-urgent, which he reviews on the train home. He jots instructions in the margin, and returns them to her the next morning. Pat handles the remaining e-mails herself, summarizing her actions for him.

Gaston Caperton, CEO of the College Board, has a good system to keep e-mail from overwhelming him. First, he reviews his e-mail throughout the day—a few here and a few there, as time permits. But he also has a terrific backup tactic, by ensuring that his assistants are aware of what is most important to him. So he can go for several hours without looking at e-mail and not feel pressured, because his staff will regularly check his e-mail and bring to his attention any critical matters.

TO PRINT OUT OR NOT TO PRINT OUT?

Some people work well handling e-mails directly on the computer, while others work more efficiently by printing them out, especially long ones. But if you have an assistant, though it seems counterintuitive and Ludditish, printing out is a terrific timesaver.

Tim, a manager at Nickelodeon, as a test, handled seven or eight e-mails on his computer in the usual way, and then printed out the next seven or eight. Of the printed group, he replied to two himself, and jotted handwritten notes of instruction to his assistant on the rest and passed them on to her. (In TRAF terms, that's a "Refer.") Handling the printed-out group took Tim only half the time it took to take care of the computerized e-mails!

Wayne Forehand of the Florida Power Corp. finds it timesaving, when he's on the road, to ask his assistant to print out his e-mails and fax them to him at his hotel, where he works through them in the evening.

SORTING AND PRIORITIZING E-MAILS

To make it easier to prioritize his e-mails, Jonathan Pond, president of Financial Planning Information, uses several e-mail addresses, one for top priority clients and consultants who need a quick response; one for less urgent matters, such as queries through the company website; and a third for personal messages.

Prioritize incoming e-mails by sight via color-coding: red for your boss, green for top customers, purple for your spouse and other personal messages.

Formatting e-mails for clarity and speed.

Jenette Fetzner, vice-president/National Accounts at CIGNA, has developed two markers that characterize an effective e-mail:

Keep e-mails crisp by following the "fifteen-second rule": Let the recipients know in the first few lines the "nut" of the letter. Do you want them to call you? Attend a meeting? Pass on the results of a sales trip? The "nut" should not take the reader longer than fifteen seconds to read.

When directing an e-mail to your direct reports: (a) summarize the action required; (b) designate the lead person; (c) provide a date for follow-up; and (d), when appropriate, designate a separate follow-up date for your assistant.

An additional tip: Save readers' time and speed responses by numbering or bulleting the main points in your message rather than sending out a block of undifferentiated text.

WHEN AND HOW TO HANDLE E-MAIL

Dennis Bass, deputy director of the Center for Science in the Public Interest, Washington, D.C., says, "I don't like being faced with fifty e-mails when I come in to the office, so I check my e-mail from my computer at home in the morning while I'm making coffee."

In a 2002 profile in *Business 2.0* magazine, Martha Stewart says, "I stay in touch, but on my schedule. [I get about thirty to one hundred e-mails per day, and] e-mail is the last thing I do at night and the first thing I do in the morning . . . I am a very fast reader and I answer everything that's appropriate."

At Bessemer Securities, some executives look at their e-mail in "deliveries" three times a day: in the morning, after lunch, and at 4:00 p.m.

To keep from getting distracted by arriving e-mail, disable the alert sound, and put your calendar or something else on the screen so you don't see e-mails arriving.

My personal tip: Take a half hour to unsubscribe from e-mail newsletters, Listservs, and so on, that you've lost interest in; remove your name from distribution lists you don't need to see. And always zap without opening any unfamiliar or "come-on" e-mails—and protect against viruses.

Managing E-mail Follow-up

Carol Gregor, AVP/National Accounts at CIGNA, drags e-mail awaiting a response to the "Task" folder in Outlook Express, and gives it a due date. Each day she double-clicks on her Task folder, and that day's follow-up e-mails appear. (Caution: you cannot drag attachments.)

Faye Davis, corporate vice-president of Facilities at Sprint, keeps her e-mails in her in-box until they are resolved. For example, the day we spoke, the person in charge of an upcoming corporate offsite had sent her five FYI update e-mails, which she would keep in her in-box until the offsite was over. Once resolved, these informational e-mails are either, in TRAF terms, "Tossed" or "Filed."

Bronwyn Clear, Exploration Manager for Kerr-McGee Oil & Gas Corporation, uses her "Sent" box as a follow-up tool—keeping *only* those messages she plans to follow up on. For example, she sent the preliminary agenda for a meeting to six associates, requesting their comments. After a few days, Ms. Clear checked her "Sent" box and found that two hadn't responded, so she followed up to ensure she received the comments in a timely way.

HOW ONE MANAGER GETS PEOPLE
TO RESPOND TO HER E-MAILS

Leeanne Probst-Engels, AVP/National Accounts, CIGNA, developed an effective four-step method for getting people to reply to her e-mail requests for information: Kill 'em with kindness. "To get people to do what I need them to do in a [non-reporting] relationship, my approach is 'Let's find a partnership solution!' The *problem* is the enemy, not them."

1. Probst sends her initial e-mail with an auto-reply request.
2. If her e-mail has been opened but she didn't get a reply, she sends a second e-mail. "Do you need more information?" Most of the time the second e-mail does the trick. If not:
3. Probst goes to the one-two punch of e-mail plus phone call, calling the recipient, repeating, "Do you need more from me?"
4. If there is still no response and the recipient is in her building, she'll go in person. She rarely has to repeat the process. The kindly but firm continuous pressure isn't something people want to go through more than once.

The E-mail Quandary:
Balancing E-mail with Personal Contact

When is it better to phone or to talk to someone in person, rather than e-mail? I was surprised by the passionate *negative* responses from numerous executives ranging from middle managers to CEOs, who express three points of concern about e-mail as a means of communication: it eliminates human interaction and nuance; it is an inappropriate means to convey complex or controversial information; and it is inefficient.

Akira Chiba's favored tool of communication is personal contact—by phone or in person—rather than e-mail. His reasoning is that "communicating in real time gives you the chance to exchange not only the subtleties and nuances of information, but also the subtleties and nuances of emotional tone."

That point was seconded by Gaston Caperton, CEO of the College Board, who pointed out, "You can bring people out more in person, and get the information you need, both one-on-one and in a group. In addition, I learn things I could never learn through e-mail."

The strongest negatives were expressed by Leonard A. Lauder of Estée Lauder: "I hate e-mail. I will never use e-mail if a personal visit or phone call can be done. I think business is all about face-to-face interaction."

In fact, on the theory that it's productive to insist on a little human interaction, one of the Estée Lauder companies has a "no e-mail Fridays" policy. Mr. Chiba, in the same vein, strongly encourages his employees to *talk to*, not e-mail, each other.

The answer to this debate may lie in sorting out whether the communication is a straightforward question or FYI, or whether it is complex or nuanced. For example, say at 2:00 p.m. your boss asks you for sales figures by close of business, but you must get a direct report to provide them.

Ask yourself, "Am I more likely to get a good outcome if I send an e-mail saying, 'Please send me these figures by 4:00 p.m.'? Or would it be better to show some consideration by sticking my head in that person's door, saying, 'I'm so sorry to ask you on such short notice, but Sue just asked me to get these figures'?"

On the second point, Faye Davis, who is in charge of all Sprint physical facilities and property nationwide, expressed concern that "people tend to write an e-mail instead of picking up the phone for a matter that's at all controversial or has any complexity."

A cardinal rule for e-mail is that you should never convey sensitive, controversial, or emotionally intense material, unless you want the whole world to read it. As a case in point, Neal L. Patterson, CEO of Kansas City, Missouri–based Cerner Corp., learned this lesson the hard way. He created a needless firestorm by sending an angry e-mail to 400 managers, expressing outrage at the "lagging work ethic" of company employees. "I will hold you accountable. You have two weeks. Tick, tock."

The e-mail was soon posted on Yahoo! Patterson's dire warning and furious tone caused such tumult that Cerner's stock price plummeted 22 percent in three days.

The rule of thumb of Dennis Bass, deputy director of the Center for Science in the Public Interest, is that if he receives an e-mail longer than three or four paragraphs, he'll stop reading and call the person. "It's easier to talk than to type—and when e-mails get too long, then you're spending way too much time in nonproductive typing." Bass also believes that complicated issues are not appropriate for e-mail. "When you're getting e-mails responding to a point that was made two e-mails back, then it's time for a conference call."

On the third point, several executives mentioned that a simple phone call can accomplish in three minutes an exchange of information that could take seven or eight e-mails.

Consider this imaginary script between an advertising vice-president and one of his account executives. Face-to-face or e-mail? Which is more efficient?

VP: Paul, what's the status of the comments you'll make at tomorrow's presentation?

Account exec: All set!

VP: How did you decide to present all the demographic info we discussed? On a slide or in a printed report you'll distribute?

Account exec: I decided a slide would be enough.

VP: Well, I think it might be best to include them in the report, too—on separate pages at the back, if that's easier at this point.

Account exec: No problem. I can print all that out and insert it.

VP: Sounds good. Could you e-mail me the final draft?

Account exec: Sure. I'll get to it first thing after our staff meeting. Look for it around two o'clock.

When you consider the high distraction quotient of e-mail, it seems that often a quick phone call or a chat in the hall is a net-plus alternative—a situation in which both parties win.

So powerfully did many executives express themselves on the necessity of establishing a clear distinction between "the facts, ma'am," for which e-mail is completely appropriate, and more-complex levels of communication, that I call it Organizing Law No. 4:

ORGANIZING LAW NO. 4:
Never use e-mail when
a verbal discussion is more efficient.

The idea here is e-mail balance: make sure e-mail is balanced with personal contact, either face-to-face or by phone. Establish your own balance, which is critical for managerial effectiveness as well as practical concerns.

One CEO's E-mail Advantage

According to a story in the *New York Times,* when Louis V. Gerstner took the helm at IBM in 1993, the company was in such desperate straits that employees at every level felt free to send him e-mails, totaling in the hundreds, "giving candid assessments of IBM's problems and even advice for the new chief." Gerstner replied with an e-mail to all employees, acknowledging their ideas and themes. He cited painful layoffs, noting, "You've told me that restoring morale is important to any business plans we develop. I couldn't agree more."

Evidently, Gerstner felt that this e-mail onslaught was a terrific grassroots tool, and took employees' counsel to heart. In his e-mail he promised to spend much of the next few months traveling to IBM factories and offices, talking to workers.

Fast-forward to Gerstner's retirement in 2002, when he had, by most people's lights, "saved IBM." He had followed through on his e-mail promise, and his tours to IBM installations were credited by many as the opening salvo in checking IBM's downhill slide.

Without Gerstner's immediate access to opinion and concern throughout the organization by way of e-mail, he might never have had that open channel that allowed him to "take the pulse" of the company and know the first steps he needed to take.

E-mail Endpapers

FAQs

Q.—Our group coordinator will often e-mail the same request for action to three or four of us simultaneously. So all of us are working on the same task—talk about duplication of effort! How can we avoid this?

A.—Ask the coordinator to send a request for action to only one person at a time—but spread the requests out evenly, perhaps by using the alphabet: First Alice, then Derek, then Joe . . .

Q.—Some of my staff have become careless about checking for e-mail messages from me. How can I encourage them to be more alert?

A.—First be sure you're not bombarding them, being verbose, or using e-mail to convey difficult news. Assuming those caveats don't apply, here's what one clever manager did, according to the newsletter *Manager's Edge:* He sent everyone an e-mail saying they could leave early on a Friday. When he strolled through the building late that Friday afternoon, he found several employees still there because they hadn't checked their e-mail. From that time forward, they checked it regularly.

Q.—My team's e-mails tend to be too long and rambling. How can I encourage conciseness?
A.—Establish a "no-scrolling" rule. If a message requires scrolling down, it's too long. If material is simply too long to fit on one screen, have it sent as an attachment.

Summary of Five E-mail Rules That Executives Live By

1. To reduce people in the loop, ask this question: If you had to photocopy this material, put it in envelopes, and stamp and mail it, who would be on your distribution list?

2. Follow journalistic style: Put head points at the top, then follow with detail.

3. Summarize information to date at the top of a long string of e-mails.

4. Adopt a "no-scroll" rule: All messages should fit within one screen. Send longer materials as attachments.

5. Try to fit the whole message into the subject line: "Meeting at 3:00 p.m. Thursday is on." "I'll be in Chicago on Th & Fr . . ." "Could you pls print out last month's marketing SS [spreadsheet] when you have a chance?"

PART II

THE TOOLS
OF SUCCESS

• • •

How Successful Executives Get Organized
Through To-Do Lists, Calendar/Planners,
the Telephone, and Technology

3

The To-Do List

• • •

A KEY TIME-MANAGEMENT TOOL

The famous mantra devised by Napoleon Hill, author of the "success" classic *Think and Grow Rich,* says, "Plan your work and work your plan." It's a good rule that almost every successful executive follows. The key to the "planning" part is an effective, workable to-do list.

Ivy Lee's $25,000 To-Do List

There's a great old legend that illustrates that point. According to the story, Charles Schwab, founder of the Bethlehem Steel Company near the beginning of the twentieth century, was approached by a man named Ivy Lee.

Lee, who was both a pioneer in the field of public relations and something of a hustler, said, "Mr. Schwab, I'd like to give you a simple time-management technique. Try it for three months and then send me a check for whatever you think it's worth—and if it's not worth anything, don't send me anything."

Three months later, Schwab sent Lee a check for $25,000. And that was back in the days when a dollar was a dollar. What was Ivy Lee's $25,000 secret? A disarmingly simple formula:

1. Make a limited list of tasks to be completed each day—about ten.

2. Prioritize the list in descending order from 1 through 10.

3. Start with 1, then tackle 2, and continue on in order.

4. Don't fret if you don't finish. You will have spent your day on top priorities and can accomplish the rest another day.

And now, for a nominal sum, we will reveal how an executive's choice of the appropriate task-list format enables her to work at the top of her game.

Three Executive To-Do List Styles

Here's an interesting productivity wrinkle: I found that different executives add to their personal productivity matrix by identifying the to-do list style that best suits them. One manager's high-powered, detailed to-do list is another person's slog through the mire. The canny manager figures out what works best for him or her.

I've observed three distinct executive to-do list styles:

- The high-powered, detailed to-do list, organized on a daily or weekly basis.
- The "rolling" master list—a single to-do list, updated, revised, and rewritten on a more or less daily basis.
- The minimalist to-do list—just a few items, scratched on Post-its, an index card, or a legal pad.

The High-Powered, Detailed To-do List

Many people who use this type of list design to-do list forms that they carry with them through the day and week. Leonard Lauder's form (see page 52–53) resides on his assistant's computer. As a task comes up, including follow-up on phone calls, etc., he'll ask his assistant to enter the task on his to-do form on the day he plans to take action on it.

Then each morning his assistant, Jeanie Janiro, will print out that day's to-do list, and he'll work through the tasks à la Charles Schwab as time permits during the day.

Marty Edelston of Boardroom Reports and Gaston Caperton of the College Board both prefer to-do list blanks, printed on letter-size card stock, which they fold up in number-10 envelope lengths, jotting notes and updating them throughout the day.

A few of the tasks on Marty Edelston's list are:

discuss health care organization oppty with Brian
schedule a meeting with attys to wrap up contract
review results of aggressive outside list testing

But how do you know whether this kind of detailed, heavily task-oriented list is the right style for you? Because it seems to be linked to an intensely hands-on form of productivity.

For example, Marty Edelston to this day wears two hats, CEO and "final editor." He also personally continues to develop advertising and marketing ideas. With these multiple responsibilities, keeping track of everything becomes a challenge, so a complex to-do list—priority tasks, general tasks, who he needs to see, phone calls, etc.—is a necessity.

Gaston Caperton expressed the view, "I don't think a good executive today is one who just manages other people. I'm the quarterback, not the coach. I'm out there on the field. There are jobs you do yourself. So you manage those jobs *and* make sure you are giving people what they need."

Is this your to-do list style? Are there clues that hint that you are, by temperament, a hands-on manager for whom this kind of

MON. FEB 14	TUES. FEB 15	WED. FEB 16

To Do
Saturday
February 19

Saturday
February 19

January

Su	Mo	Tu	We	Th	Fr	Sa
						1
2	3	4	5	6	7	8
9	10	11	12	13	14	15
16	17	18	19	20	21	22
23	24	25	26	27	28	29
30	31					

February

Su	Mo	Tu	We	Th	Fr	Sa
		1	2	3	4	5
6	7	8	9	10	11	12
13	14	15	16	17	18	19
20	21	22	23	24	25	26
27	28					

March

Su	Mo	Tu	We	Th	Fr	Sa
		1	2	3	4	5
6	7	8	9	10	11	12
13	14	15	16	17	18	19
20	21	22	23	24	25	26
27	28	29	30	31		

April

Su	Mo	Tu	We	Th	Fr	Sa
					1	2
3	4	5	6	7	8	9
10	11	12	13	14	15	16
17	18	19	20	21	22	23
24	25	26	27	28	29	30

May

Su	Mo	Tu	We	Th	Fr	Sa
1	2	3	4	5	6	7
8	9	10	11	12	13	14
15	16	17	18	19	20	21
22	23	24	25	26	27	28
29	30	31				

June

Su	Mo	Tu	We	Th	Fr	Sa
			1	2	3	4
5	6	7	8	9	10	11
12	13	14	15	16	17	18
19	20	21	22	23	24	25
26	27	28	29	30		

This is the custom designed computerized form used by Leonard A. Lauder for his tasks and appointments.

THU. FEB 17	FRI. FEB 18	SAT. FEB 19
		SUN. FEB 20

Appointments
Saturday
February 19

July

Su	Mo	Tu	We	Th	Fr	Sa
					1	2
3	4	5	6	7	8	9
10	11	12	13	14	15	16
17	18	19	20	21	22	23
24	25	26	27	28	29	30
31						

August

Su	Mo	Tu	We	Th	Fr	Sa
	1	2	3	4	5	6
7	8	9	10	11	12	13
14	15	16	17	18	19	20
21	22	23	24	25	26	27
28	29	30	31			

September

Su	Mo	Tu	We	Th	Fr	Sa
				1	2	3
4	5	6	7	8	9	10
11	12	13	14	15	16	17
18	19	20	21	22	23	24
25	26	27	28	29	30	

October

Su	Mo	Tu	We	Th	Fr	Sa
						1
2	3	4	5	6	7	8
9	10	11	12	13	14	15
16	17	18	19	20	21	22
23	24	25	26	27	28	29
30	31					

November

Su	Mo	Tu	We	Th	Fr	Sa
		1	2	3	4	5
6	7	8	9	10	11	12
13	14	15	16	17	18	19
20	21	22	23	24	25	26
27	28	29	30			

December

Su	Mo	Tu	We	Th	Fr	Sa
				1	2	3
4	5	6	7	8	9	10
11	12	13	14	15	16	17
18	19	20	21	22	23	24
25	26	27	28	29	30	31

intensely detailed list would be suited? Check off any of these three characteristics that apply to you:

- ☐ Pleasure in discrete tasks that have definite beginnings and endings.
- ☐ An interest in how things are made. Perhaps in earlier years— or even now, as relaxation—you enjoyed tinkering with autos or the innards of computers.
- ☐ A taste for exactitude in knowing where projects stand at any given moment.

If you checked two or three boxes, this suggests that intense task involvement will release your productivity.

ONE EXECUTIVE'S HIGH-POWERED TO-DO LIST

One interesting and unusual high-powered to-do list is that designed by Marcia Zerivitz, founder and executive director of the Jewish Museum of Florida, in Miami.

Because Ms. Zerivitz is the final decision-maker on all matters pertaining to the museum, floods of queries, tasks, and decisions are literally and figuratively dropped onto her desk all day long.

Her tasks might include writing a thank-you note to a donor or planning negotiations with the city around cutting down a tree on the historic property of the museum grounds.

To get a grip on all this, Ms. Zerivitz divides her to-do list into the nine major categories she's directly responsible for: board development, administration (staff and the "business" of running the museum), building issues, financial, fund-raising, museum collection and programs, marketing and PR, communications, and their current expansion effort.

Each evening before she leaves, she works through all the papers that have accumulated on her desk, together with all her notes and jottings. For example, if someone has, during a call, asked her to do something, she'll capture it on a sticky and incorporate it into her list. Never, never would she trust her memory.

"I always tell people," she says, "if you don't see me writing it down, tell me, because it won't get done otherwise."

Ms. Zerivitz composes tomorrow's to-do list organized by category. For example, under "staff," an item might be "Talk to the curator about two things he needs to focus on." Under "board" might be a reminder to call a board member who specifically requested that she call him tomorrow.

These are her priorities, the things she knows she has to get done the next day.

Ms. Zerivitz composes the list on the computer, but prints it out and updates it as she goes through the day. When she goes out, she tucks the list into her Day Runner. She'd never be without it.

"My favorite thing is when I can take things off the list," she laughs.

A highly structured to-do list tends to reflect a highly structured mind—someone for whom the task of organizing the discrete "bits and bytes" of tasks is the currency of the realm. So the fundamental time-management principle of the day is ways and means of accomplishing tasks.

The two other styles of executive to-do lists—the "rolling" list and the "minimalist" list—are simpler, with less variation from one executive to another. But, interestingly, the simpler lists represent a complex attitude toward time, in which the "productivity markers" of the day are less focused on tasks—though of course they must still be accomplished—and more focused on interaction with others.

The "Rolling" Master List

A "rolling" master list is simply a continuous list to which to-dos are added constantly as they arrive.

SEVEN VARIATIONS ON THE "ROLLING" MASTER LIST

1. *The "slips of paper" tactic.* Katharine Graham, the late chairman of the Washington Post Companies, whom I had an opportunity to interview several years ago, worked with her assistant to create a master list by assembling masses of jottings. "I have a list that I prop up on the inkwell. And the list does get done actually."

To capture all the ideas and reminders, Mrs. Graham kept pads by all the phones in her house, and on the desk, and would make a note when something came up. All those notes were given to her assistant, who assembled them into Mrs. Graham's to-do list. If it was an idea Mrs. Graham was not ready to act on yet, she put the note into her own "inner file" on the left side of her desk to be pulled out at a later date.

2. *The steno pad method.* Here's how executive recruiter Millington McCoy, managing director of Gould, McCoy & Chadick, works from company offices in New York and Florida, according to Carol Hymowitz in a *Wall Street Journal* profile:

"She carries a three-page memo of current projects, updated weekly, that includes all the names and numbers she'll need. McCoy also totes a steno pad where she jots her plans, notes calls she's made, and checks off completed tasks. This pad, she says, 'is nothing sexy, but I can flip through it on planes and in cars, keeping track of everything I'm doing.'"

3. *A single master list.* To prevent "to-do-list overwhelm," an extensive master list needs to be broken out into "current" and "do later" items.

One executive, Joy Soto Kocar, president of Integral Solutions, a Colorado-based technical writing company, says the concept of a master to-do list helps her tame her extremely busy life. Kocar broke out her master list as follows:

a. Record in a single master list every idea, call, project, or task as it arises, large or small, minor or important. (Always keep your master list instantly available, on paper, PDA, or desktop computer.)

b. Review the master list daily, dividing large projects into manageable components.

c. Compile a daily list of ten tasks to realistically accomplish each day, ranked in order of importance (à la Charles Schwab). List at least one "high payoff" activity each day.

d. Schedule high-priority items during your most effective time of day.

"Having a prioritized master list of the goals you need to accomplish really helps put things in perspective," Kocar says.

4. *The dictation method.* One time-pressured head of a firm in New York's fashion industry keeps adding phone calls to make, memos to write, and ideas to follow up on to his to-do list, while crossing out accomplished items. At the end of the day he dictates his list to his assistant, specifying due dates and order of priority. His assistant types up a fresh list and puts it on his desk each morning.

5. *The index cards technique.* And here's how a district sales manager for a medical instruments company has taken control of his time by using index cards:

a. He enters each task on an index card, along with due date and an estimated time allocation, e.g., "Review three proposals; due next August; two hours." He stars priorities in red.

b Every morning he pulls six task cards from his stack: two or three high-priority tasks, the rest of average importance.

c. He slates priority tasks for the morning hours, when he's freshest.

d. At about 4:00 p.m., he completes whatever outstanding tasks he can, and reassigns any task not finished that day to another day.

When someone asks him for a few minutes, the district manager can honestly say "I've got an important appointment (with my priorities). Can we talk later?"

6. *The tickler-file based to-do list.* Nancy L. Lane, retired VP/ Community Relations at Johnson & Johnson, organizes her action system by date. She sets an "action day" for each item on her agenda, enters the specific tasks on her schedule, and then puts any background materials in a tickler file that she refers to on the scheduled day. If circumstances change and she can't get to it after all, she simply reschedules the task and returns it to her tickler for another day.

7. *Mind dump.* In his book *Getting Things Done: The Art of Stress-Free Productivity,* David Allen describes an interesting approach to setting up a weekly to-do list: He calls it a "mind dump on paper." On a pad or in your PDA, write every task, goal, and would-like-to-do that comes to mind. Then divide the tasks into two categories: those that you can or should delegate, and those that *you* must do. For each task, note the steps that you or those you delegate need to take during the coming week, and a time for starting each step. Then monitor your list each day. A good "mind dump" time is at the end of the work week or on Sunday evening, so you can look ahead to the coming week.

See also the review of priority-based to-do lists in chapter 11, Managing Multiple Priorities (page 145).

The "Minimalist" To-Do List

Interestingly, and counterintuitively, a substantial number of executives work with extremely spare to-do lists.

GOOD IDEA: A TO-DO REVIEW

In his autobiography, Lee Iacocca wrote that every Sunday evening he worked through his past week's to-do list to see what had and had not been accomplished, and then set up his working plan for the coming week.

Each day, quickly scan your to-do list as follows:

1. What's the worst that could happen if this task was postponed or dropped altogether?
2. Assuming it must be done, is the task appropriate to my level of responsibility? Can it be delegated as a whole or in part?
3. Can the task be simplified, made less detailed, or otherwise downsized?

Gerard R. Roche of Heidrick and Struggles, executive recruiter extraordinaire, tries to write down each day, before he goes to work, a brief "top task" list—the five or six most important things he wants to do each day. "This kind of business defies the well-planned, organized approach to things, which is all the more reason to be that way."

Verna Gibson, in her days at The Limited, also focused her attention on no more than five or six items daily.

Arthur Levitt is even more casual. He just jots the odd item as it comes up on the "schedule card" he carries with him as he goes through his day. When he returns to his office, he and his secretary work through his notes, putting them into immediate action.

So the minimalist to-do list—which many high-level executives use—couldn't be simpler or more basic. But its very simplicity gives rise to an interesting question: How is it possible to successfully manage major responsibilities with a few reminders jotted on a card or yellow pad? There's a fascinating answer to that question. But let's table the discussion of the implications of the very short and often casual executive to-do list for now, to be reopened in our discussion of executive time management in chapter 14.

SIX STEPS TO "WORKING" YOUR TO-DO LIST

Creating an attainable daily plan—one that you can usually complete despite interruptions—will allow you to go home every day with a sense of accomplishment and renewed focus. Follow these six steps, developed by Peg Pickering in her book *How to Make the Most of Your Workday,* to work your list:

1. Write down everything you want to accomplish during the day.
2. Seek out items you can delegate. Assign them immediately.
3. Note any task with a specific deadline directly on your calendar.
4. Assess each remaining task according to its estimated time commitment and difficulty: high, medium, or low.
5. Allocate each task a specific time during the day—keeping your energy levels throughout the day in mind. Don't overbook, as unexpected developments will surely impinge on your plan.
6. Move any uncompleted tasks to the next day's to-do list. Don't try to pack it all in. Always be realistic about how many tasks you can reasonably hope to accomplish each day.

Career-Building Advice

A good working to-do list is a map, a navigational plan. The executive key to productive use of the plan is (1) to sequester yourself for a half hour to an hour a day to work on top-priority tasks, and (2) to stay on high alert, seeking out even five-minute intervals to forward tasks, a little at a time. With this one-two punch, you will arrive at your goal.

Is there a fear to be faced in order to accomplish the "win"? Oddly enough, a fear many people face is the fear of succeeding at consistently accomplishing the tasks on their to-do lists. This is a genuine accomplishment. It means conquering the fear of being an effective person. Should that kind of fear be getting in your way, dig down deep, face your fear, acknowledge your right and ability to be effective, and plow right in to get those suckers done!

SEVEN WAYS TO ACCOMPLISH SOMETHING BIG IN TWO MINUTES OR LESS

Do little vacant capsules of time slip unexpectedly through your fingers during a typical day? It's amazing how much you can accomplish by filling in with worthwhile activities those two minutes to kill before leaving for lunch, for example, or while waiting for the call you're expecting at ten o'clock. Here are seven little "flash tasks" you can accomplish in two minutes or less:

- *Pick up the phone and confirm a meeting time.* Just say, "I'll be there at two o'clock next Tuesday," and ring off.
- *TRAF one or two items from your in-box.* Taking a "flash" opportunity here three or four times a day can make a big difference.
- *Dictate a short memo onto tape—or directly to your assistant.* You'll get much more dictated in two minutes than you might expect.

(cont'd on page 62)

**SEVEN WAYS TO ACCOMPLISH SOMETHING BIG
IN TWO MINUTES OR LESS** *(cont'd from page 61)*

- *Proofread a one-page or two-page document.* This is not a task that requires the ten or fifteen minutes we usually set aside.
- *Get a quick briefing on work-in-progress from a team member.* On the phone, by e-mail, or in person, this is a highly effective "flash."
- *Delete two or three older files from your computer.* "Flash" here twice a week and quickly clean up your hard drive.
- *Thank a staffer or assistant for capably handling something yesterday.* Staff encouragement can be just a "flash" away.

4

The Art of the
Calendar/Planner

• • •

When Arthur Levitt sets out on his rounds of meetings and appointments, his entire calendar consists of nothing more than the day's schedule typed out by his secretary on an index card, which he carries in his pocket for instant retrieval. "I always buy shirts with pockets for that reason," he explains. If something comes up during the day he wants to record, he'll jot it on the card and follow up on these items with his assistant.

By contrast, Dr. Julie Flagg, head of a thriving multiple-physician practice in Wesleyan, Connecticut, is a Palm devotee. Other executives, such as Brian Kurtz, executive vice-president of Boardroom, Inc., would feel at a loss if shorn of their thick Day Runners or Franklin Planners.

For top executives, their calendar/planner is more than a calendar—it's "action central," a vital productivity tool enabling them to get a hold on time. Their calendar/planner—with all its prompts and stored information—is the navigational map that guides their days.

Although executives express their individuality more in their selection and use of calendar/planners than in almost any other area of time management, the critical commonality I discovered was that, just as with paperwork and phone calls, top executives are extremely disciplined in the daily processing of their calendar/planners.

This dedication is one of those valuable CEO hallmarks that you can easily develop, no matter what your own responsibilities. Disciplined processing is divided into four parts:

1. Choosing the calendar/planner that is most effective for you.

2. Entering all follow-ups and "working" information as they arise.

3. Faithfully checking your calendar/planner every day.

4. Acting on any and all prompts in your calendar/planner.

If your calendar/planner is to fulfill its function, you must faithfully perform the four tasks listed above. The ability to do so effectively, though, is predicated on choosing the right style for yourself. So we begin there.

Choosing Your "Keep It All Together" Tool

Clients often ask me which style of calendar/planner I think is best. In my early days as an organizer, I would advise people which calendar to use based on what worked for me. But over the years I've found that people's calendars are as individual as fingerprints.

My study of senior executives confirmed my conclusion that no one "CEO" style of calendar/planner exists. It varies from the barebones approach—e.g., schedules typed on a sheet of paper or card, à la Arthur Levitt—to highly complex guides to life. The lesson here seems to be that an organized calendar that you process every day is essential, but the methodology and mix—paper and electronic— varies widely.

When it comes to your choice of this valuable tool, the good news is that all calendar/planner roads lead to Rome. The question is, how do you want to get there?

People often complain to me that they have trouble finding time each day to keep their calendar/planners shipshape. In my experience, that problem is not caused by some great failing on their part, but is rather the consequence of choosing the wrong type of calendar/planner for the way they work.

For starters, ask yourself these three questions:

1. *Are you involved in long-term projects involving multiple meetings and complex due dates?* If so, you may prefer a manual calendar/planner like the Franklin Planner. While somewhat heavy to tote, this gives you ample room to take and keep notes in a central place, and track multiple tasks and priorities. Or you may simply prefer this style because it affords you the ability to keep track of everything you're working on, in detail, in one reference tool.

2. *Do you work on the go, with more of a day-to-day orientation (such as sales, where you have a lot of appointments)?* If so, you might choose a calendar/planner that is light and easy to work with, like a Day-Timer or a PDA.

3. *Do you have a complex work/personal life schedule that needs to be integrated on a real-time basis?* If so, a PDA you can carry everywhere—even to your kid's soccer game—may be the best alternative.

To help you further define the type of calendar/planner that will be most effective for you personally, take a minute to fill out this questionnaire:

CHOOSING A CALENDAR/PLANNER

What sorts of materials do you keep, or would you like to keep,
in your calendar/planner?

TYPES OF MATERIALS	YES	NO	If no, where do you keep these items (e.g., a notebook for voice mails, for example)?
Follow-ups, items to track and monitor			
Brief "minutes" and action items arising from meetings specifically with your manager			
Brief "minutes" and action items arising from other meetings and appointments			
Task lists			
Action items you have delegated and/or passed on to others			
List of phone messages			
Goals, immediate/short-term			
Goals, long-term			
Addresses and phone numbers			
Birthdays, anniversaries, staff anniversaries, card and gift reminders			

If you checked three or more items in the "yes" column, or if you indicated that you don't have satisfactory "homes" for three or more items, then a full-service planner—as opposed to a pocket calendar like Akira Chiba's (page 72) or a simple "week-at-a-glance"—might be just the ticket.

ELECTRONIC TIP

If you would like to digitize a handwritten address book into your computer to be printed out for your calendar/planner, but your assistant can't read your handwriting, dictate it!

Read the contents of your address book into a recorder, and let your assistant transcribe the tape. That would not only get those handwritten names and numbers into the computer, it would allow you to edit out older addresses and add pertinent information where necessary, as the taping proceeds.

No-Frills Versus Comprehensive Planners

When I first started to explore the time-management systems of senior executives, I wondered whether they had some special kind of complex calendar/planners, especially devised to manage their complicated schedules. Instead, I discovered that most executives have adopted one of two basic methods, based on their working styles and temperaments. The good news is that both styles work, so as you read along, when you instinctively feel that one is you, go with it!

The "No-Frills" Calendar

Frankly, I was surprised at how many top executives like Arthur Levitt use only the simplest, most bare-bones schedules on index cards. We may live in a digital age, but many CEOs prefer to stick with the basics.

As with Mr. Levitt, Jeanette Wagner, retired vice-chairman of The Estée Lauder Companies, carries a blue schedule card prepared by her assistant. Ms. Wagner uses the card as her expense control, writing down taxi, lunch, and other expenses. Once back in her office, she staples the receipts to the card and gives everything to her assistant to process.

Leonard A. Lauder, chairman of Estée Lauder, uses a variation on this theme. His assistant prints out his daily schedule in reduced size and inserts it into a stand-up Lucite photo frame on his desk so it's completely visible all day, which is helpful in keeping him on track. He takes an extra copy with him when he goes out.

Now, I'm the first to admit that the reason many CEOs can operate on this simple calendar/planner system is that they have assistants who manage their calendars for them. A journalist I know who regularly interviews CEOs told me that in her experience, executive assistants almost always set up the appointments because their bosses are so busy all day that they don't have the time or the inclination to figure out when they can meet or talk with someone.

That said, an assistant's authority to make appointments on behalf of the executive can range widely, from making all appointments to making none. Since you may not yet have a full-time assistant to schedule your appointments, if you want to adopt the simple "card" version when you're out and about, you might have to combine a regular calendar/planner at your desk with the index-card version to carry around so you can keep on top of it all!

Faye Davis uses a system that falls somewhere in between. Her assistant uses the online calendar MS Scheduler, keeping it constantly updated. "Handling my calendar is my assistant's primary responsibility," says Ms. Davis. "There are lots of meetings, lots of changes. She has to know what to do if the CEO calls. She has to know who to say no to, or pass someone on to." Her assistant prints out the day's schedule, which Ms. Davis keeps on her desk, and carries with her when she goes out.

Sandra Kresch, formerly a partner at Booz Allen and now an independent consultant, says that one of her assistant's great contributions is assembling all the detailed info and backup materials Ms. Kresch needs for the day.

ONE EXECUTIVE'S CALENDAR-MANAGEMENT STRATEGIES

Teodoro Benavides, city manager of Dallas, Texas, makes a point of regular calendar review. He says, "I ask my secretary every Friday to give me my calendar for the next three months. I'll review it over the weekend and make changes: 'Oh, those days are too full. I'll need time to dig, so I'll need to open them up.' Or, 'This is a really big issue coming up—so I'll need to allocate more time to prepare.'" In that case, he'll ask his secretary to reschedule some appointments to open up the time he needs. What's interesting is that he is very aware at all times of his need never to let his appointment calendar become too jammed up, so he is always able to react flexibly.

Ms. Kresch says, "When [my assistant] leaves in the evening, I have a detailed calendar of what the next day will be, and whatever backup I need. If I am interviewing, there are résumés attached. If there's a board meeting, I have board minutes attached, etcetera. And it has addresses if I'm going out and about, and if I'm going to the airport, who is going to pick me up and who's going to take me and whatever. Everything is extremely well organized."

Even if you don't have an assistant to do this, the concept is a good one. Try gathering all the information you'll need related to each appointment or meeting the night before and placing it with your calendar so you can grab it quickly and go!

The Comprehensive Calendar/Planner

Now we come to the other side of the spectrum: the full-blown calendar/planner that contains your entire life, either in one book or on a PDA.

WHEN TWO CALENDARS ARE BETTER THAN ONE

Like many corporate leaders, you may be on the go all the time, traveling, attending meetings outside of the office, etc. This can lead some people to keep two calendars to stay on top of a moving target. Again, the preference is up to you.

My studies indicate that most executives use a single, unified calendar for both business and personal activities. One professional, Mary Farrell, with the New York State Department of Education, makes the point that whether the commitment is a corporate meeting or getting your son's tricycle fixed, time is time, and everything should go in the same place.

On the other hand, Marcia Zerivitz of the Jewish Museum of Florida prefers two calendars, noting that "I have two Day Runners . . . I just got used to writing things down in both places. I have a big one that sits on my desk and that has everything. If I've asked the curator to have something ready by Thursday, I'll put it into the [desk] Day Runner . . . All the daily notes go there, things I have to remember."

The smaller Day Runner that Ms. Zerivitz carries out and about emphasizes reminders of tasks she must do herself—errands, phone calls to make out of the office, a matter to discuss with someone at a chamber of commerce luncheon.

Today, many executives use different media for their two calendars—perhaps a paper calendar in the office and a PDA on the go.

The idea of a comprehensive book as a daily navigational tool took hold in the 1980s with the rush to Filofaxes, Day-Timers, and the ubiquitous Franklin Planner. Since that time the concept has taken on digital form in the Palm Pilot and similar products.

How do executives and managers use these comprehensive-style planners? Jenette Fetzner, vice-president/National Accounts at CIGNA, feels that her ability to operate successfully day-to-day is heavily predicated on her comprehensive calendar/planner, which includes not only appointments but phone and voice-mail listings and ongoing projects.

Another executive who combines appointments, tasks, and reminders on the same page is Ronald Goldsberry, chairman of OnStation Corporation, a leading provider of Internet-based channel-enabling technology. "I have a little book in which I plan my own day in terms of either phone calls that I need to make or messages that I want to communicate to someone or reminders for myself. It's a Day-Timer. I've used that for, I guess, about the last fifteen years." Mr. Goldsberry captures everything in his Day-Timer, including, say, an issue brought up by a manager that he wants to keep track of.

ONE EXECUTIVE'S POST-IT TIP

Bill Dugan, an executive at Briefings Publishing Group in Alexandria, Virginia, relies on his manual calendar. When someone makes a tentative appointment or he needs to follow up on an issue, instead of writing that item in pencil on his calendar, he sticks a one-inch Post-it on his calendar on that spot. If he needs to change the date, he can simply move it around as circumstances warrant, and only write it in once the item is finalized as to a date or time.

If you're someone who likes to keep everything, including long-term goals, in one place for easy reference, then the more comprehensive-style calendar/planners will work best for you.

Manual or Digital? A Hot Debate

Opinion is divided among executives about the use of Palm organizers versus paper calendars.

As Marcia Zerivitz points out, you have to know how you function best. She continues to prefer a manual calendar—in her case a Day Runner. "I have to see the paper," she explains. "I have to see it written down. That's the way I function. I don't think I'll ever [go to an electronic device]." She's often amused when making an appointment with someone who adroitly pecks away on a PDA, only to enter it incorrectly. "They always show up on the wrong day. I say, so much for the PDA. They can't get their calendars to work."

Even though Pokémon is a technologically sophisticated company that creates interactive software, Akira Chiba, its U.S. president, prefers to use a pocket-sized manual calendar in which he notes not only appointments but items he wishes to follow up on, phone numbers, brief "minutes" of meetings, and the like. He doesn't even own a PDA.

Then, in the opposite camp, you have Dr. Julie Flagg, head physician of a large OB/GYN medical practice in Wesleyan, Connecticut, who is a big Palm fan. Dr. Flagg wears two hats, as CEO of her multiple-physician practice and an active practicing physician. Managing her multiple responsibilities means that her "keep it all together tool" is of primary importance. "I thought I'd go to my grave with my Filofax," she insists. "But the Palm was an incredible advance for me. I wear it on my belt. I have it with me all the time." She lists the following items as those she keeps on her Palm:

- addresses
- her list of ongoing projects (about seventy)
- people to phone today

- "waiting for" ("For example, if I told you I wanted your thoughts about this conversation, I'd put that prompt in 'waiting for.'")
- a communications list ("A spot for my partner Beth, a spot for my office administrator Linda . . . so when I see Linda, I will just hit that button and see what I want to tell her.")
- protocols ("If you're pregnant and diabetic, there are certain protocols that must be followed.")
- a "next action" list ("For example, after one of the staff meetings, if there's something I'm supposed to do, I put it in my 'next action' area.")

The primary factor that prompted Dr. Flagg to go electronic was the availability of an updated digital medical reference on pharmaceutical drugs. Once she decided she needed that, the transition was inevitable. And, of course, she can sync her Palm with her computer.

Another time multiplier: she learned Graffiti in a few hours, and prefers it to scribbling things in her Filofax because of the necessity of going slower. She thinks it forces her to focus more on the subject at hand. Interesting.

If, like her, you're a person on the move, and always have the Palm on your belt, that's another multiplier. Whatever you've entered is there for good, so you don't get that panicky feeling, "Oh gosh, where did I put that?"

Dr. Flagg sees only one downside to the Palm: she can't view her whole week at a glance, which she had on her desk on the Filofax calendar.

Despite the many advantages of going digital, there appears to be a mini-trend of sticking with, or reverting to, manual calendars from electronic calendars. And I have found many executives who like their manual calendar, and are sticking to it, electronic age or not.

One executive—a regional sales manager for a medical instruments company—confessed to me that he had switched back. For years his Franklin Planner had been a completely dependable navigator in which he recorded every task, notes from meetings, every phone call and follow-up.

But persuaded by colleagues to "join the twenty-first century," he switched to a PDA. Then the trouble started: he began missing deadlines because he couldn't enter information into the PDA quickly enough.

When he suffered a serious embarrassment by failing to set up a series of meetings his manager had requested because he hadn't gotten it into his PDA, he switched back to his old calendar/planner, observing, "It was like greeting a long-lost friend."

A woman at one of my seminars, where we were debating this issue, provided a succinct framework to determine in which cases a manual or electronic planner might be preferred—which didn't involve being an unregenerate Luddite.

As a sales manager, she felt that her PDA was her lifeline to her staff and customers. Her PDA was primarily a *reference* device—who was doing what, and where—and also a *connectivity* device.

If schedules needed to be changed, or if she wanted to set up a conference call with her team that afternoon, she communicated this through their PDAs. The only rule was that everyone on her team had to check their PDA every half hour unless they were with a customer.

On the other hand, this woman's husband, who was very computer-savvy, continued to use a Day-Timer because he emphasized a different set of uses. His planner was primarily a *capturing* device and *memory prompt.* Although the sales manager also used her PDA for notes and jottings, in her job those were a subordinate use. For her husband, it was a primary use. His calendar was "Houston Central" for all his information.

If you're still unsure whether to go digital, take a minute and fill out this short questionnaire:

	Yes	No	Digital or Manual?
Do you simply enter a list of appointments, with little or no additional info?			Manual or digital is okay, but digital is probably simpler to use and maintain.
Does your schedule need to be coordinated with others on a regular basis?			If yes, definitely digital.
Do you enter substantial info into your planner over and above your schedule?			If yes, probably a manual calendar would be your tool of choice.
Are you a real expert at using Graffiti or another handwriting PDA tool?			If no, with substantial entries, you would certainly use a manual calendar; if yes, a PDA might well do the job.

No matter which style or format you adopt, the key to effective time management and efficient functioning is a comfortable and automatic spot to (1) capture the necessary items and (2) address them promptly.

As CEOs can tell you, *the habit that makes all the difference—that makes these simple tools work—is daily processing,* which is necessary to make your work flow smoothly and accomplish all your tasks. When follow-ups and the rest are neglected, you end up in a workload quagmire!

Four Quick Tricks to Optimize Your Calendar/Planner

1. In a PDA, use bold or italics to identify priorities or such special-focus items as assignments from your boss. In a manual calendar, use highlighters.

2. If you go manual, soften the irritation of writing in birthdays, etc., each year by creating a separate "birthdays and anniversaries" list that you—or, even better, your assistant—can use as a guide to entering them into your calendar. Enter a prompt at the beginning of each month to buy that month's cards, prepare and stamp them, and just pop them in the mail on the right day.

3. Manual users: To protect yourself from the horrors of losing your planner, keep a backup set of addresses and any permanent records in your computer. At the beginning of each week, photocopy that week's entries plus those for the next two weeks ahead. Keep major dates, such as those of the annual conference and quarterly reports, on your computer or on a separate pad.

4. Here's a treasure trove for manual users: At the beginning of each year, before consigning last year's calendar to the storage bin, page through it quickly for nuggets of useful information. You might find, for example, in notes from a meeting with your boss last March, that he had mentioned a project he'd like to undertake, but it was never pursued at that time. So you decide to mention to your boss the possibility of reactivating the idea. Or, in June last year, perhaps, there was an interesting meeting of an industry organization, but you hadn't gotten on their mailing list. So you ask your assistant to go to their website and put you on the list.

No matter what system or combination you choose, I offer this one word of advice: I've seen managers defeated by having too many working tools in too many places. So be sure to select a few that integrate well!

5

The "Capture Book" Tool: An Interesting Hybrid

• • •

One quick, simple tool that numerous managers and executives praise for saving them more times than they care to count is an ordinary notebook in which to capture random thoughts and information. It's not a to-do list, though there might be to-do items in it. It's not a schedule or calendar, though there might be items in it that will be calendared.

The "Capture Book"

Basically, to use David Allen's phrase, it's a "mind dump," a single repository of all those odds and ends of information that we tend to put on yellow stickys or scribble on envelopes. But executives who use the single book—what I call the "capture book"—keep all the over-the-transom bits and pieces in one place, usually in a dedicated notebook.

People use their books in different ways. For some it's a simple record of phone numbers or brief reminder notes, while others use their notebooks as "idea books" in which to capture future possibilities.

Lucette Kirbach of the Legal Services Society of British Columbia says, "I keep a notebook next to my telephone. Every morning I date a new page, and during my workday every message, request, reminder, address, telephone number, etcetera, is briefly written down. Once I have dealt with the item, it's checked off with a small date beside the item." This notebook has been a lifesaver to Ms. Kirbach many times.

William Bratton, Chief of the Los Angeles Police Department, and former New York City Police Commissioner, who is widely credited with the dramatic drop in crime in New York on his watch, has a variation on the "single notebook" theme.

He moves around a lot during the day, visiting outposts of the extremely far-flung LAPD. To make sure he captures, say, a matter that a precinct captain might ask him to look into, or a request for a copy of his book *Turnaround: How America's Top Cop Reversed the Crime Epidemic*, or a phone number, he carries a few small pads with him to jot such items down, never trusting to memory.

Chief Bratton said ruefully, "The bane of my existence is that I have not mastered the art of having one book. I see so many people very skilled at that."

But back in the office, he'll sort through his notes and jottings, toss those that don't make the cut, and personally write those for which he wishes to retain a record into a spiral notebook he keeps on his desk.

Chief Bratton will launch any tasks or initiatives his jottings suggest, or simply have a handy place to keep a phone number or brief record of a conversation that he might want to flip back to a few days later. He's found his book to be a valuable reference and prompt.

Richard Branson, founder and chairman of Virgin Atlantic Airways, also counts a notebook among his favorite working tools. He has 122 black notebooks he's filled over the years. "I can't believe when I see people not writing things down," he says. "You know they aren't going to remember everything."

For example, when Branson travels on Virgin Atlantic, he writes down lists of things he wants improved, such as seats that aren't reclining properly or a wheelchair-bound passenger who had to wait too long for assistance.

Karen Settle, founder and president of Keystone Marketing Specialists in Las Vegas, who carries a letter-size spiral-bound notebook/phone log, uses colored highlighters—red for action, yellow for appointments, green for family—to easily identify the items that she needs to keep track of.

Ms. Settle, who fills one notebook every month or so, says this simple tactic captures everything chronologically and in simple diary fashion. It also prevents her (usually) from scribbling notes and phone numbers on stray pieces of paper.

My own editor has told me she finds it useful to separate to-do's from more substantive notes in her notebook. "I use the right-hand page of a spiral notebook to write down all to-do items (everything from writing flap copy to sending an e-mail to my boss) and phone messages. The left page I use to record notes from a phone conversation or from a meeting. So I have both the substantial information and the more mundane to-do's in one book, but separated by the pages the material is written on."

The idea of capturing important ideas and insights in a single place—a sort of "possibilities notebook"—was a theme for several executives.

Larry Alterwitz, the head of Walker Furniture Company, a family-owned business in Las Vegas, got the idea, which he entered into the notebook he keeps on his desk, of setting up a "marketing calendar" of his competitors. He suggested that his company start keeping track of when their competitors changed their window displays, what their themes were, when they introduced different advertising concepts at different times of the year, different types of ads, and so on. He said,

"You are running your own horse race, and at the same time you know where your competitors are and what they are trying out."

Martha Stewart is quoted in *Business 2.0* magazine (June 2002) as saying, "I never discard an inspiration. When I travel, I always pack spiral blue notebooks, one for every month. I use them to jot down my thoughts and I never throw them away."

Carl Menk, former head of the executive recruiting firm Canny, Bowen, keeps a notebook at his bedside to capture any middle-of-the-night thoughts. However, he concludes somewhat ruefully, most of his night thoughts are not worth following up. Says Menk, "The productivity of my 3:00 a.m. notes is about 30 percent." I think that's not bad!

Variations on the "Capture Book" Theme

Index cards. The "capturing" tool of choice for some people is index cards.

Anne Lamott, author of *Bird by Bird: Some Instructions on Writing and Life,* lives by her index cards, which serve her as a rich source of ideas and insights.

"One of the worst feelings I can think of [is] to have had a wonderful moment or insight . . . and then to lose it," she confesses. So she keeps index cards and pens all over her house and carries a pen and card in her pocket whenever she goes out to capture every idea and observation.

"If I'm working on a book or an article . . . I paper-clip [the cards] to a page of rough draft where that idea or image might bring things to life." When her writing stalls, she looks through her index cards for inspiration.

"I believe in lists and I believe in taking notes, and I believe in index cards for doing both," Lamott says.

An "ideas" folder. Marcia Zerivitz of the Jewish Museum of Florida uses an "ideas folder" in lieu of a notebook. Explaining how she uses the folder, Ms. Zerivitz told how her museum had set up a new tier—an advisory council. Their first meeting was held theater-style, but a few of the people said, "You know, it would be really helpful if next time we could sit around a table and see each other." So she jotted that suggestion on a pad and threw it into her folder.

"You can't do everything that everybody suggests," Ms. Zerivitz cautions. But she reviews that folder regularly and makes an effort to implement fresh ideas that are feasible.

Dictation. One "tech" alternative to the ubiquitous notebook, for those who have access to transcription services, is dictation. A favorite strategy of James Kerasiotes, former chairman of the Massachusetts Turnpike Authority, is to capture his ideas by dictating memos, notes, and to-do's into a small tape recorder that he carries with him everywhere, for later transcription by his assistant.

Marty Edelston of Boardroom, Inc. followed the same practice, and then asked his assistant to print out each individual item on distinctive green paper, which then became a "working stack" for ideas and initiatives to launch—or toss.

An updated version of the dictation concept is voice-recognition software. Robert J. Giordano, head of MRB Investor Relations in New York City, believes his whole decision-making process has been upgraded by his ability to explore options using Dragon Naturally Speaking software (see box on page 82).

But for the time being, the old standbys of pen and notebook seem to be the tools of choice for capturing thoughts, random facts, and reflections. And some people even have a "magic pen." One executive has told me that he uses a particular fountain pen, and that for some reason his ideas and thoughts seem to flow much more freely than when he uses any other writing implement. He misplaced it once for a

DICTATION REDUX—A CLASSIC TIMESAVER

That classic timesaver—dictation—is making a comeback thanks to a leading-edge voice-recognition software.

Even though dictation saves loads of time over typing, people still seem unfamiliar with its advantages.

To Robert J. Giordano, CEO of MRB Investor Relations in New York, the ability to dictate, without a secretary, using Dragon Naturally Speaking Software, has multiplied his efficiency.

Benefits: Giordano dictates all kinds of material, but he feels the software especially shines in situations where "speaking dialogue" is helpful: scripting a conference call with clients, for instance, or role-playing a challenging meeting such as a meeting with union representatives or prospective investors.

Another benefit—quite unexpected—was an improved decision-making capacity. Giordano found that he wasted less time and could respond more rapidly to any issue if he dictated his thoughts.

One incredibly convenient touch: There is also a portable dictation product available that you can keep in your car, dictate as you drive, and then download as you would a Palm.

Getting started and logistics: Giordano found that it took about one half hour of "coaching" for the software to recognize and respond to his voice. He read it *Alice in Wonderland!*

At that point, accuracy was about 75%, but rose quickly after regular use to 90%+. Handling proper names could be annoying, but if the names are used regularly, once corrected, the software will "remember" them.

Punctuation and style elements are simply spoken in: comma, period, double space.

Once a document is entered into your system, emendations can be typed, and the document can be corrected or revised just as with any other document.

Downside: The only downside Giordano found with the system is that, because you're wearing a headset, dictation is awkward when people are popping in and out of your office. So it's best to use the system at a quiet time when you can concentrate.

week, and confessed that he felt somewhat at a loss. Fortunately, the pen was recovered and it made all the difference to him.

It's almost impossible, except for people who are extremely adept at Graffiti, to do this kind of free-form jotting down of ideas and facts as they occur into a PDA. When tablet computers and voice recognition software are truly ready for prime time, digitization might take over.

The lesson we can take from CEOs is the importance of developing a reliable "capture" system for yourself—because no one can be expected to remember and keep track of everything.

6

Executive Effectiveness Through Technology

• • •

Jodi Forlizzi, assistant professor of human-computer interaction and design at Carnegie Mellon University, came up with an excellent anti-interruption device. She rigged a sensor device to her office door and linked it to the Web, so that students can check on her availability. When her door is open, her website invites students to stop by. When her door is closed, students know that she's not available.

Jodi Forlizzi's device isn't on the market, but it's a good example of how one professional addressed the issue of interruptions in the workplace head-on and chose a technological solution.

Gadget Masters

One gadget master is Stephen Carter, CEO of Cingular Wireless. Mr. Carter's goal seems to be the ability to operate in a completely wireless environment, untethered from his desk. Where he goes, his work goes too. His philosophy is, "If you don't learn everything about how your technology works, you'll never be able to make your technology work for you." Carter clips a BlackBerry to his belt to handle e-mail, and carries a range of cell phones almost as accessories. On the day of a *Fast Company* interview published in the October 2002 issue, he was wearing a slick red Nokia on his belt, he carried another Nokia to use between meetings, and, for evening, he showed off a sleek silver Motorola. Carter's laptop—continuing the "mobility" theme—is an ultrathin Compaq. Yet his wireless world is twinned with an awareness of interaction with others. "You make a contract when you make an appointment with someone. I'd never let technology distractions abuse that time. I always turn my cell phone and pager off during meetings." He was not amused when a young adviser's pager went off, twice(!), during the interview.

Anne Altman, an IBM managing director, oversees all IBM's business with the U.S. government, which is IBM's single biggest customer. With all the zeal of a convert, Altman's tool of choice is instant messaging.

"Instant messaging has made the biggest difference for me. When I'm on a sales call and the customer needs a status update or a piece of information that I don't have on hand, I just send a message to someone on my team, and I get an answer on the spot.

"I received a call yesterday from a senior executive in the federal government who needed some of our white papers," recalls Altman. "While we were chatting, I shot a message to Brien Lorenz, our e-government and enterprise-transformation consultant. He sent me a bunch of files, which I forwarded to the customer—while he was still on the phone, explaining what he needed.

"Sametime [Lotus Sametime, produced by IBM subsidiary Lotus Development Corporation] allows me to have instant meetings by bringing several different people into a chat spontaneously," says Altman. The only requirement is that they all be online.

"And I can say, 'Let me draw a picture to show you what I mean,'" she adds, referring to Sametime's tools for incorporating diagrams, audio, and video into chats.

When used properly, instant messaging can be a time multiplier.

However, some managers find it intrusive when overused. If you haven't yet tried instant messaging, you might consult with your IT people and experiment with this cutting-edge tool.

Meeting Virtually

Virtual meetings are a functional choice for several "tech-wise" executives.

Meetings by computer. Stephen Carter of Cingular uses the Web to communicate with staffers all over the world. Each month he conducts a webcast with a different employee group. For example, when he conducted a webcast with the Cingular team in Puerto Rico, the chat site was projected onto a large whiteboard. Staffers at the chat site pounded out their questions, which Carter and others attending could read from the whiteboard. He verbally answered some thirty questions over the course of an hour, which a team of crack typists captured and posted to the chat site.

Another form of computerized communication that is much more accessible to the average worker is the weblog. A weblog—or "blog" for short—is a type of website that originated as a platform for personal commentaries on technology, politics, or whatever inspired the originator. Only fairly recently has the business world discovered blogs.

If you're involved in a major team project, here's another time multiplier: Set up a project blog so that everyone can have access to the latest information and can coordinate their efforts.

For example, Cisco Systems launched a cluster of "project forum" blogs a couple of years ago on its intranet. Each blog provides meeting minutes and updates on a particular project. Project engineers, marketing teams, and other interested parties can access these blogs and add their comments and questions.

"It allows us to post meeting minutes quickly without worrying about HTML, which you'd have to do with a web page," says Brian

Junnila, a Cisco product marketing manager. "Also, anyone new to a group can catch up [by reading the blog] without someone having to forward him or her a hundred e-mails."

Videoconferencing. The law firm Greenberg Traurig installed a PC-based, TV-quality system linking all of its offices.

"To fly someplace for a one-hour meeting can cost you a whole day," explains Jay Nogle, director of Legal Systems and IT point man, in an article by David T. Gordon on www.cio.com. But with the new system, clients can have a videoconference in a matter of minutes without losing the sense of trust they get from "seeing their lawyer."

With all the reluctance to travel since 9/11, videoconferencing is catching on even more than it had before. Videoconferencing even had a role in moviemaking: Director Barry Sonnenfeld, who lives in the East, telecommuted during the making of *Men in Black II*, which was released in the summer of 2002. With digital technology he could use a dedicated videoconferencing satellite to go over work in progress for *MIBII* with the special-effects firm in California.

"They can see me, I can see them, and most important, we can both look at the film that we're working on," Sonnenfeld said in *Business 2.0* magazine (July 2002). "We both have a tablet with an arrow, and I can circle areas and say, 'Here it's looking a little too dark.'"

Eric Richert, Sun Microsystems teleconferencing expert, suggests these strategies for ensuring the success of your videoconference:

Have participants at each location sit on one side of a rectangular conference table. On the other side of each table, place a monitor that displays the attendees sitting at the conference table at the other location. That serves two goals: (1) It will appear that attendees at both locations are in the same room, sitting at one table; and (2) each attendee can see the gestures and expressions of those at the other location.

Make sure all attendees are working from the same handouts. "That way," Richert explains in *Fast Company* magazine, "both groups are looking at the same information, everyone can understand what's going on, and no one gets confused."

Wendy Miller, VP/Marketing for the Boston consulting firm Bain & Co., says that, given a choice, she prefers videoconferencing to audioconferencing.

"In a videoconference," Miller points out, "you can see people's reactions. I find the ability to be in visual contact, even long distance, keeps everyone alert and in touch.

"And besides," she says ruefully, "I know that during audio conferences, people are checking their e-mail while talking to you."

Meetings by telephone. Candace Petersen, VP/Corporate Marketing and Strategy for digital-projection industry leader InFocus, based in Wilsonville, Oregon, works with developers who are scattered across the world—in the Netherlands, Norway, and Singapore. She holds two kinds of regular long-distance meetings with them by telephone. The live meeting is a twice-a-month conference call. Petersen shifts the times of the call to make sure that everyone spends some time in the midnight slot.

The other telephone meeting, held weekly, is delayed-action, and is conducted by using voice mail. "I . . . send out," says Petersen, "what I call 'assumptive' group voice mails where I lay out our challenge for the week and ask for input on particular issues or projects." Petersen's staff is asked to respond within twenty-four hours with comments.

More Ideas on Conference Call Meetings

- Dallas-based Chancellor Media, one of the largest owners of radio stations in the United States, keeps its far-flung program directors in touch with monthly conference calls in groups of eight to ten program directors sorted out by format—urban contemporary, Top 40, country, etc. As a value-added feature: An outside expert is frequently invited to "address" the phone conference on a topic of general interest.

- Richard Brown, CEO of EDS, created new ways to drive accountability and cooperation. In the monthly "performance call," for example, he, his COO, and his CFO began hosting Monday-morning conference calls of the company's roughly top 150 leaders. These calls are essentially an ongoing operating review, in which the company's performance for the previous month and the year to date is compared with the commitments people have made. The calls provide early warning of problems and instill a sense of urgency. The calls can be uncomfortable for those in the negative column. In front of their peers, executives have to explain why and what they're doing to get back on track.

- Twenty of DuPont CEO Chad Holliday's top managers are stationed around the world. To keep them informed, Holliday holds biweekly conference calls with the group. His four goals for each call are to gather the intelligence he needs; to keep his managers abreast of changes in customers, competitors, local economics and politics; to provide a forum for managers to share their insights with one another; and to help them develop a seasoned global perspective.

  To engender thoughtful responses, Holliday always asks pointed questions: "What's happening to your customers and to their customers?" "How are politicians handling economic conditions in your part of the globe?" "Should their actions have any effect on us and on what we are doing?"

  "By hearing simultaneously from their peers," Holliday says in an article by Ram Charan in *Fortune*, "[our top managers] broaden their perspective of the global landscape."

Certainly these conference-call meetings are not confined to CEOs. For example, Peter Vandevanter, vice-president of the New Ventures Division of Knight-Ridder in Charlotte, North Carolina, felt that weekly meetings with his editors were vital.

However, since two of the editors would have to commute one hour each way, he now holds these meetings via audioconferencing, reserving the right to call people in when necessary. The editors were immensely grateful for this consideration.

More Executive Tech Strategies

PDAs and Hand Computers

Dennis Bass, Deputy Director, Center for Science in the Public Interest, recommends as a useful tool a PDA tied together with an e-mail system, which makes it easy to convert e-mails into tasks and appointments, or peg them to a particular date, or cut and paste them into a memo.

Michael Treschow, the CEO of Electrolux, and his wife, Charlotte, Investor Relations Chief at Skandinaviska Euskilden Bank AB, do a lot of personal communicating by way of their PDAs. The two used to give each other handwritten itineraries for the week. Now they share a calendar between their PDAs that contains all the information they need to know. Internet service providers such as Yahoo! offer to subscribers such software as shared calendars.

Other Favored Executive Tools and Techniques

Stephen Paolicelli, Quality Assurance Manager at DMV International, has installed software that allows him to read news and other online services on his PDA. "It comes in handy when I'm waiting in the doctor's office or the car-repair shop" or when he has five minutes between meetings. This is an example of making good use of those stray ten- to twenty-minute stretches you might find in your day. Technology provides good ways—through PDAs, e-mail news alerts, etc.—to stay informed and to gather information on the fly.

PORTRAIT OF A "WIRED" EXECUTIVE

Gregory L. Summe is an example of a twenty-first-century "wired" executive.

"There's an expectation now for CEOs to be much more in touch with customers, employees, and investors than in the past," says Summe, head of PerkinElmer, Inc., a Wellesley, Massachusetts, maker of laboratory instruments and airport X-ray machines.

While traveling, Summe's "staying in touch" tools include a cell phone, his PC—to check market updates and refine his multimedia presentations—and a sophisticated financial calculator.

At home, his communication options include two cell phones, four phone lines, a fax machine, and a cable modem for high-speed Internet access. Ironically, Summe says his traditional Day-Timer is still the best calendar/planner for him.

7

Working the Phones

• • •

HOW SENIOR EXECUTIVES MAKE THE TELEPHONE A POWERFUL TOOL

John Curley of Gannett shared with me an amusing paradox about corporate success: The higher you go up the ladder, he observed, the more you call people, but they don't call you. He described a visit to a past chairman of Gannett many years ago, when he was still on the city desk of one of the Gannett newspapers. He was amazed that the CEO received no phone calls while Curley was there—whereas he knew that a minimum of five to seven phone messages had accumulated on his own desk during that time.

It is true that the higher an executive rises up the corporate ladder, the less likely his or her subordinates are to call in for casual chats. By the time Curley became CEO of Gannett, he too received fewer phone calls, but the telephone itself remained his chief interactive tool, as it is for many senior executives.

Using the Telephone Strategically

Curious about how leading executives use the telephone strategically in an era seemingly dominated by e-mail, I set out to discover tips from them that managers at all levels could use. So I posed this question to several executives: "If you were fogbound at an airport for two hours, what is the one tool you would want to have with you?" The answer, in every case, was "my cell phone." There was only one tool that every executive I spoke with defined as central to his or her ability to function effectively: not the computer, not the e-mail pager, but the telephone.

As was discussed in chapter 2, the direct contact provided by a phone conversation offers reams of information—nuance, emotional tone, the ability to question, explore, and learn—that isn't available on e-mail. You can accomplish an enormous amount by making good use of it.

As I explored how senior executives "work the phones," two key strategies emerged: Always respond; and Take advantage of voice mail.

Always Respond

The great, great majority of top executives literally cannot bear not to have a phone call returned—either personally or by someone on their behalf—within twenty-four to forty-eight hours at the most. This is a deeply embedded characteristic epitomizing the decision-making

---

TAKING "STAYING IN TOUCH" TO ANOTHER LEVEL

Vanguard Group CEO John J. Brennan devotes considerable time to staying in touch with customers—literally. He regularly snaps on a headset and, from a cubicle in the customer service department, fields investor calls about everything from fund prices to current yields to the company's trust services. This hands-on technique helps Brennan find ways to constantly refine and improve his company.

As the second-largest mutual-fund company, Vanguard must be doing something right. It is rapidly gaining on longtime number-one player Fidelity Investments.

imperative. This insistence on returning calls is one of the reasons these people have arrived at the top, because they can be relied upon.

Former SEC head Arthur Levitt makes a practice of calling back *anyone* who calls him, no matter who it is, within twenty-four hours—including calls from strangers. He's curious—and talking to people gives him a sense of trends and of people's concerns.

Brian Kurtz, executive vice-president of Boardroom Publishers, will even return, or ask his secretary to return, sales calls. Kurtz has a kind of "philosophy of relationships": what you put out there will flow back.

That personal "bulldog" imperative to respond and reach closure—which was discussed previously in the context of paperwork and e-mail—applies equally to phone calls.

So insistently do virtually all senior executives feel the obligation to return calls promptly that this qualifies as an organizing law:

ORGANIZING LAW NO. 5:
Return all phone calls within twenty-four hours—personally or through a staffer.

Here are some "always respond" strategies:

Howard J. Rubenstein, the legendary New York PR representative to the stars, says he has never failed to return a phone call in forty-five years. Here's how he manages his phone calls:

His secretary prints out a list of the one hundred calls he receives on average during the day. At home in the evening, Rubenstein color-codes them in red, yellow, or green by priority level, and returns them in that order.

Arthur Levitt asks his secretary to make a list of people to call, and he calls them all at once, one after the other, until he has plowed through the entire list.

Delegating phone calls to staffers is also a key component in executives' skill at fast turnaround. Here are some of their strategies:

Gaston Caperton of the College Board will return most calls the same day, but if he's really rushed, he'll have his assistant call and say, "Gaston will call you, but next week."

Bill Little, Pekin Insurance sales manager, counts heavily on his assistants to help him manage phone calls. "They have great judgment," he explains. "If I am needed, they will find me. Otherwise, they handle as many calls as possible."

Mary Rudie Barneby, of UBS Financial Services, Inc., says, "Phone calls from people I don't really know, or that I know to be lower priority, I give to the people who work for me, and ask them to follow up."

When Seth Gershel, former head of Simon & Schuster's Audiovisual Division, assigned a staffer to an author's project, he would check with the author to make sure that his staff member was returning phone calls promptly and was generally "on the case."

Take Advantage of Voice Mail

If you don't have an assistant to help you make and follow up on calls, using voice mail—when you know a person has left the office or is at lunch—is a good way to quickly return calls and convey key information without getting caught in long chats you may not have time for. That's acceptable, but be sure to keep your messages as brief and succinct as possible.

Think of voice mail as simply another kind of "mail," like e-mail and postal mail. You can handle voice mail efficiently and effectively, too, with the TRAF (Toss, Refer, Act, File) system. Here's how:

Toss = Delete.
Refer = Forward. Pass on a client request to a staffer to respond, for example.

Act = Action. Returning the call is your most likely action, but perhaps another action is required, such as looking up some information online.

File = Archive. If a voice-mail message outlines the main provisions of a contract and you don't have the paperwork before you, archive it until you have the hard copy to compare it to.

Here are two additional tips: To avoid delay and backup, don't listen to a voice-mail message twice. TRAF it right away. Many voice-mail systems have a function that speeds up the message when you listen to it; that can be a real timesaver.

Some never-fail strategies:

Todd Cowgill, Regional Claims Manager, Pekin Insurance Company in Pekin, Illinois, writes down voice-mail messages as he goes through the day in a "dedicated" notebook used only for that purpose. He takes advantage of any intervals to return phone calls and e-mail— if possible that day.

A top executive at Kerr-McGee facilitates his own rule of returning calls within twenty-four hours by dividing his stack of messages into two piles: "Call back ASAP" and "Call back after hours." He has

---

TWO VOICE-MAIL TIPS

- Slide your message list into your planner on your way out the door so that you can return calls during meeting breaks, in a taxi, or at other in-between times.
- In general, when you are overloaded with voice-mail messages, it's a good strategy to have your assistant or an intern type them up on a call sheet so you can go down the list and return them at a convenient time.

learned that after-hours calls—which usually entail simply leaving a message—are a lot easier to keep brief and to the point.

One CEO made this promise on his own voice mail: "I'll respond to your message within the next day. If I cannot get back to you within that time, my administrative assistant will call you with a response or a time by which I can respond directly."

I can't stress enough how important it is to fulfill that pledge. Not only is your credibility on the line, but you risk holding someone up or interrupting the flow of a project if you aren't responsive.

How Not to Be a Slave to the Phone

Peter Bohacek, in a letter to the editor in the *New York Times*, suggests giving out only your land-line phone number. Then, when you want to be reached, have those calls forwarded to your cell phone (with caller ID if you wish to be selective). Calls you don't take will go into a single voice mail—that of your land-line phone.

Teresa Oliszewicz of CUNA Medical Group, Madison, Wisconsin, felt a compulsion to check her voice mail whenever she saw her red indicator light flashing, so she cleverly covered up her indicator light, and now can work undistractedly, checking her voice mail only at certain times of day.

Low-Tech Phone Directories

Martha Stewart says, "I have laminated lists of all my personal and business phone numbers, which I keep by every phone. You don't want to know how many phones I have. I also have lists in my car and in my purses. I carry them with me instead of a Palm. I find it infinitely faster. My assistants update and laminate new sheets once every three months."

The phone is a great tool. Use it well, intelligently, courteously, and strategically—and *always* return calls—and you will maximize your productivity and get the benefit of voice communication that e-mail doesn't afford.

PART III

EXECUTIVE TIME AND TASK MANAGEMENT

•   •   •

8

The Organized Executive's Day

• • •

One manager said to me, "You know, we've never been trained in how to organize the day. We're overwhelmed—there's so much on our plates."

That we know. But the question that preoccupied me is this: Are CEOs overwhelmed? How do they organize *their* days? What does an organized day look like at the top? And what can managers and professionals at every level learn from them?

Well, many senior executives have found an excellent and fascinating way to find their own way.

The Executive Time Shift Strategy

If I were to ask the average manager about his or her notion of what an organized day looks like, most people would say, "I'd have a lot more control than I do now. I'd do thus-and-such at nine o'clock and thus-and-such at ten," or "I'd be able to close my door for a good part of the day so that I could get a lot more things done."

Most people assume that because they dream of organizing their day by controlling it, that must be what CEOs actually do. But this was one of my biggest surprises: The working premise of a CEO's day is that time is fungible. Their emphasis is not on controlling their time; instead they focus on controlling what they can accomplish throughout the endless changeability of the day.

The lesson the executives can teach us is how to shift our perspective on what an organized day actually is. The CEO's view of an organized day is essentially the opposite of most managers'.

ORGANIZING LAW NO. 6:
Gain power and productivity
by managing, rather than trying to control,
the changeability of the day.

The vitality, and even the excitement, of their working days is achieved through a combination of the following elements:

- *A private "on your own" hour for priority tasks.* Carving out that vital "sweet spot" of time that is essential to personal productivity.
- *Calendared meetings and appointments.* Imposing a skeleton structure, outside of the "sweet spot" hour, on an ever-shifting day.
- *Unstructured, free-form time.* An attitude toward the unstructured part of the day that allows them to perceive it as positive and energizing rather than negative and intrusive.

Strategies to Gain Your
Personal Priority Hour

Is there an optimal time of day to claim your priority hour? Absolutely. Most people are on high alert in the morning, while some people are at their best in the afternoon. The goal is to slot your most challenging work into the hours when you are best up to its demands.

Taking Your "Sweet Spot" Outside Office Hours

Early morning or late at night quiet-time strategies. Some believe, along with the eighteenth-century theologian Matthew Henry, that "those who would bring great things to pass must rise early."

Robert A. Iger, president of Disney, gets up at 4:45 a.m., goes to the gym until six o'clock, then goes to his office and reads until his first meeting at seven. "I think people have their own rhythms," he says. "In my case, it's the morning. I'm less ornery."

Howard J. Rubenstein, head of the Rubenstein Associates PR firm, is in his home office by 4:30 a.m. flipping through TV news programs. Then he works through color-coded files he's brought home, prioritizes the calls he needs to return, signs checks, and reviews his calendar. After his work session, he stretches and goes for a run.

Don Imus, broadcaster and gadfly, "begins thinking about how to ruin someone's life" when he awakens exactly at 4:17 a.m.

Jeanette Wagner of Estée Lauder saves routine administrative work, such as signing letters, expense reports, etc., for the end of the day when she is tired. Says Wagner, "If, on the other hand, I have to solve a problem—either a people issue or a conceptual one like working on the general managers' conference—that can sometimes mean I take my private time on the weekend when I don't have interruptions, or it can mean early-morning time."

But sometimes 3:00 a.m. is a creative time of day. "I don't need a lot of sleep," Wagner says. "I often wake up in the middle of the night and take out my pad, and I know that I must put [the idea] down then . . . Sometimes I can solve a problem or outline an entire project in an hour that may have been giving me a problem before."

It's likely that the idea of getting up at 5:00 a.m. is daunting and beyond expectation. But if you normally get up at six-thirty, try waking up a half hour, then an hour, earlier. Most people find that they can shave off some sleep time without paying a terrific price, and the benefits you get—more work done, perhaps achieving a less frenetic pace during the day—can be huge and enduring.

The quiet commute. Another outside-office-hours quiet-time strategy is the quiet commute. While many senior executives and CEOs gain focused time because they have the use of a driver to take them to and from work, you can get (almost) the same effect in two ways:

1. *Public transportation.* Mary Rudie Barneby of UBS Financial Services, Inc., says about mornings, "In the morning I'm very productive . . . I get on a train and I will take a stack of paperwork and just get through it. I have about an hour and twenty minutes, so it's really good time."

The most wholesale timewaste of all time, which I frequently observe as I leave Manhattan in the early morning to go to the airport, is the endless line of cars at a standstill on the other side of the Long Island Expressway (known locally as "the world's longest parking lot") going into Manhattan.

Why, I've asked myself, do people tolerate that frustration and timewaste, when they could be putting their time to much better use on the train than sitting there honking their horns? Beats me.

The truth is that many commuters have the option of taking a train or a bus to work, instead of driving their cars. What you gain in productivity from quiet, focused time on a train is probably well worth whatever you give up in convenience and independence. Think about it.

2. *The "quiet time" carpool.* Consider putting together a carpool of local commuters who might be interested in adapting a popular Washington, D.C., practice known as "slugging," in which commuters, strangers to each other, wait at prearranged pickup points where cars stop by to take them into the city in order to take advantage of the fast-moving "multiple-passenger" lanes.

TIME JUST TO THINK

Finding time just to reflect seems like a luxury. Rarely do "ahas!" arrive at work, because you don't give yourself time to just think. These two executives, by taking time out during their day, gained fresh perspectives and, no doubt, some breakthrough ideas.

Richard "Skip" LeFauve, retired president of General Motors' Saturn Division, makes thinking a priority by actually putting it on his calendar. He writes topics he wants to mull over on his personal to-do list, and schedules time to think about them, giving them the same priority as other appointments. In addition, he calendars time to talk with trusted associates to get a fresh perspective on nagging problems.

Here's a "time-out" tip from Horst Schulze, former president of the Ritz-Carlton Hotel chain: Schulze spent a half hour every morning meditating on better ways to provide great customer service, wherever he was that day. The result: a hotel chain known for its superior service.

The message here is that (a) quiet thinking time is essential, and (b) if it doesn't come naturally during the course of your day, schedule it.

Here's the key: a rule of "slugging" is that the cars are quiet. No music, no chat, no cell phones. You can work, think, read, or relax.

Five Strategies for Gaining Quiet Time During the Office Day

1. *Disappear.* If you have the freedom to come and go during the day—if your manager doesn't start asking "Where's Gerry?" if you're not at your desk—then vanish into an empty conference room. Or take a walk around the block. Or bring some reading to the cafeteria.

A department head at General Foods slipped for about an hour a day into an empty office next door with a frosted glass window so no one could see him inside.

A lawyer in New York, after greeting everyone when he arrives, then takes the next elevator back downstairs and hunkers down for an hour at the Starbucks on the corner.

2. *Negotiate a "quiet hour" with your manager.* If simply disappearing isn't realistic, negotiate a quiet hour with your manager. The chief benefit from your manager's point of view is probably to provide you with a clearing of time in which to fully concentrate your attention on his or her priorities.

A mandated group quiet hour generally doesn't work. Too many things come up unexpectedly to put a whole working group out of commission.

3. *Stay available—with your door shut.* Most businesses have an "open door" policy, in which shutting your door is frowned upon. But at Nickelodeon, home of cutting-edge children's TV, one manager has it both ways. He installed a whiteboard and markers on his door. When his door is shut, anyone who wants to see him simply writes a note on the whiteboard. The system works because, as soon as the manager emerges, he *immediately* checks in with the people who dropped by, so they know they don't have to intrude on him to gain access.

But again the caveat: Be ruthlessly diligent about following up with people who have left a message for you. This is the only way you can make your "escape time" work for you *and* your colleagues.

Tip: What if your colleague's closed door offers no whiteboard? Keep a yellow sticky pad above the doorjamb. You will then have paper handy to write a note and leave it on the door.

4. *When you are the senior person in the group, request interruption-free time from your colleagues.* One lawyer, cited in my earlier book *The Organized Executive,* circulated this request to his office:

> After considerable thought and a great many unproductive days, I have concluded it is vital to my work that I establish a "quiet period" during which I can get important jobs done without being interrupted by telephone calls, visitors, meetings and other distractions.
>
> Consequently, I want to establish an interruption-free period of time from 7:30 to 9:00 a.m. to assist me in better and more productive use of my time. In this effort, I need all of the help that your skills, intelligence and cooperation can provide.
>
> Thank you.

5. *Leave your office an hour prior to your lunch date.* Many restaurants will allow you to sit quietly and work if you arrive on the early side, at around eleven-thirty.

Are you reluctant to claim your priority time? Many people are, even when there's no practical impediment to doing so. Many business people tell me they feel guilty about not being available to clients or colleagues for that hour.

If you've felt this concern, I'd like to help you reframe your situation by asking yourself these two questions:

1. If you were your own colleague or client, wouldn't you prefer to have your full attention? Your attention is secure when your priority time is secure. You surely know what it's like to be in that state of distraction that occurs when you can't get any time to yourself.

2. When you're in a meeting, you're also not available to clients and colleagues. How about defining your private hour as being in a critical meeting with yourself? Think of it in the same business terms that you apply to other parts of your day.

IF YOU THRIVE IN SOLITUDE, CONSIDER TELECOMMUTING

If you function optimally with long stretches of private time, you might want to consider telecommuting.

Michelle Durst, a vice-president of human resources at Merrill Lynch, moved to St. Petersburg, Florida from New York and took her job with her. She manages the company's HR website out of her home.

Her biggest surprise, as noted in an article by Lisa Chadderdon in *Fast Company* (April–May 1998): "I never realized how nice it is to work one, two, even three hours without a single interruption. In the office, I couldn't go twenty minutes without an interruption."

If the idea of spending more time in a home office has appeal, "you have to learn how to think like a telecommuter. You have to plan a day ahead, a week ahead. What are you trying to accomplish? What materials do you need? Where are they?"

You never want to be in a position where, at home, you reach for the receiver to make an important call to a client and realize you left your client's file at the office!

How Executives Structure an Ever-Shifting Day: The Checklist Solution

"I start the day with a game plan of when I'm going to do what, and right away there's an unexpected meeting or crisis, and bam—there goes my game plan. How can I get better control over my time?"

Just about everyone feels overwhelmed by the vast onrush of instant communication. A client relationship manager at a financial house told me, "What's tough is that I have a list of things to do, the phone rings with a client query, e-mails come in and and it puts me off in different directions—and at the end of the day, my desk isn't cleared. It builds up." The best-laid plans—and the best intentions— can vanish in an instant.

But once you accept the fact of interaction as reality, and no longer wish it away, *then* you can manage it, temper it, find solutions to accommodate that reality, and work within it. Here are three solutions to establishing some order and efficiency on a day that won't sit still.

The Checkpoint System

How do you "organize" a shifting day? To most of us, "organized time" is time we control. But most top executives have learned to shift away from a notion of time that entails getting things done at specific times of day, except for the priority hour, to a notion of time as infinitely elastic, with few internal boundaries.

And within that elastic time, certain checkpoints are identified and accomplished as the claims of the day permit.

There are three styles of checkpoints: functional, content-based, or mixed. For example:

Functional checkpoints

☐ Priority hour
☐ Make and return phone calls
☐ TRAF papers, e-mail, and voice mail
☐ Follow up on the follow-ups
☐ Two hours on non-priority tasks (interspersed through the day)
☐ MBWA
☐ A daily, very brief contact with each direct report
☐ A daily brief touch-base with your supervisor

Content-based checkpoints

Should you want to conceive of your checkpoints in content terms, the list might look something like this:

☐ Client contact
☐ New client development
☐ Number crunching
☐ Delegation and staff development
☐ Writing memos, letters, reports, marketing copy, strategic plans, etc.

Whatever seems appropriate. Mix and match as needed. Don't overload the circuits.

With your checkpoints in place providing an internal armature of frame and shape, *now comes the singular art that is at the root of every executive's ability to govern the free-form day:*

Reframing Time:
Mastering the "Ten-Minute Secret"

The reality, as every executive knows, is that it's a constant negotiation between your personal time requirements and the legitimate interactions of a collegial environment. This is the key to the time-management success of virtually every top executive who makes his/her way to the top of the organization. The challenge is to reframe the mental "currency" with which you think of time away from specific tasks and toward approximately ten-minute time segments.

Think of the "negotiated" day as consisting of numerous segments, roughly ten minutes each. I call them "raindrops." It's not a bad idea to invent a term—"mosaic tiles" (the term we used when we discussed this concept within the TRAF context on page 18) or "bits and bytes," or whatever—to give these ten-minute segments some metaphorical heft in your mind.

Now take this typical scenario and contrast the powerful difference in your reaction when you're thinking "raindrops" and when you're not:

You hear Marvin making his way down the corridor. You know that in about three minutes he's going to stick his head in and say, "Hey, gotta minute?" Meanwhile, you've been working for about ten minutes on plugging the final figures into the budget, and you need about another twenty minutes to finish the task. Your reaction to Marvin's drop-in is:

If your goal is to get the whole task done now: "ARGH! Interrupted again! I can't ever get anything done! My life is out of control."

If you're thinking "ten-minute raindrops": "Oh, okay, I'm about a third through. When Marvin leaves, I'll be able to get in another ten minutes before the 3:00 p.m. meeting. Then I'll sneak off somewhere for ten minutes after the meeting to make sure I finish the project up today."

Key: *You begin to think about your time flexibly and opportunistically.* This has two powerful effects: First, by drastically lessening the anger and feelings of victimization that are so widespread, because you "get it" that drop-ins and spontaneous events simply come with the territory, energies that have become blocked by resentment are released.

And, second, just the process of constantly seeking out small opportunities during the day to forward your goals, while repeatedly coming back to your checkpoint list as though attracted by a magnet, is a powerful way to gain control of your time and increase your productivity. It's a great habit to adopt, and is a key strategy that most senior executives and CEOs I know have mastered.

I'm not sure I understand why managing time flexibly and opportunistically around an organizing "pole" (e.g., the checklist) is so powerful—but powerful it evidently is, since the day of every single up-the-ladder top executive I'm aware of follows this same pattern.

Here's how this way of patterning time first came to my attention. During my visit to Joseph Vittoria, chairman, ResortQuest International, a leading vacation rental property management company, and former CEO of Avis, Mr. Vittoria had outlined on a yellow pad five or six calls he needed to make.

So he would make one call, then someone would stick their head in to ask a question or bring Mr. Vittoria up to date on something,

MEALTIME OPPORTUNITIES

Dallas city manager Teodoro Benavides makes a point of making mealtime connections. Benavides says, "Breakfasts and lunches are an opportunity to spend quality time with people I need to spend time with: employees I want to impact on, or my bosses [the mayor and fourteen councilmen], or citizens." It's a good use of time.

and he would wave them in and welcome them. Upon their exit Mr. Vittoria would make the next call, and then go pay a visit to someone on the floor. There was a veritable whirl of constant activity at a low-level hum. However, after every foray into contact with someone else, Mr. Vittoria would come back to his desk and make the next phone call. So, over a period of a few hours, his "through-line," the five or six calls he had intended to make, had in fact been made, interspersed freely among the other activities that spontaneously arose.

His day comprised a mix of structure and no-structure. This is a way of conceiving time that most senior businesspeople embrace.

With John Curley of Gannett, this same circling-in phenomenon was apparent in the way he handled his paperwork. Because Curley, as mentioned earlier in chapter 1, liked to see a substantial selection of the materials and mail that came into his office, the stack of mail on his desk was fairly high. Yet get through it he would. So the same thing happened—people would drop in and out, he'd receive multiple phone calls, impromptu meetings would occur—but he always reapplied himself to processing his pile of mail piece by piece until every item had been taken care of. Starting at about 8:30 A.M., his mail had been handled by lunchtime.

Neither Curley nor Vittoria made any effort to box their time as "phone time" or "deskwork time." Rather, they "seeded" their tasks over several hours—and completed them in timely fashion, stress-free.

So characteristic is this pattern that I would call it an organizing law:

ORGANIZING LAW NO. 8:
Seed your routine tasks throughout the day,
rather than trying to carve out blocks of time.

Career-Building Advice:
Time-Management Skills to Help You
Master the Free-Form Day

To help you master the free-form day, try adapting the following six time-management skills. We begin with Sandra Kresch, an extremely organized consultant, describing a typical day packed full of professional and personal demands on her time:

> I had a series of things to do today. My cat had to go to the vet; I had to go to the doctor; I had a very full day in the office; I'm trying to find a new executive director for a not-for-profit organization whose board I chair; and a group of friends has a set of needs that have to be dealt with.
>
> In thinking of how I would approach today, what I effectively did was work out a schedule for the whole day.
>
> The only time the cat could go to the vet was at seven o'clock this morning, so I took him and figured out a way to get him back home later.
>
> I was going to be at home for thus-and-such amount of time, and there are two business people—one in London, one someplace else—whom I've been trying to get hold of, [so I] placed the phone calls to their offices early in the morning to give them time to call me back at home before I left.
>
> My office schedule, which is always very, very tight, effectively focuses on three things that need to be done this week, and doesn't focus on anything else.

From this busy manager's recital of her day, we can discern six techniques that she employs to help her maintain some kind of control over time. I recommend them to you:

1. *Write a list* of no more than three or four major tasks you hope to accomplish during the week. Memorize the list, repeating it to yourself several times a day. Clip the list to your paper calendar or incorporate it into your electronic one where you will see it frequently. This helps focus your energy on fulfilling your weekly goals.

2. *Note the fixed points of your day*—that is, the day's armature. (The cat had to be taken to the vet early enough so it could be retrieved by the end of the day, phone calls to London usually have to be made well before noon, and there were prescheduled meetings and appointments.) Once that is outlined, you have a much clearer sense of how to fit it all in. As Andrew Grove says in *High Output Management*, "We must identify our *limiting step* . . . If we determine what is immovable and manipulate the more yielding activities around it, we can work more efficiently."

3. *Evaluate the "float" factor.* When evaluating which tasks to concentrate on, focus on those that have limited or no "float" time. For example, there is not much float on a memo that has to be prepared for a meeting at 2:00 p.m. the same day, whereas there is usually plenty of float for a meeting that will take place next week.

4. *Stretch the day at both ends.* In Ms. Kresch's example, notice the vet appointment at 7:00 a.m. Try to schedule personal errands and personal care at one end or the other of the day—say an appointment with your fitness trainer at 7:00 a.m., or haircut and grocery shopping at 7:00 p.m.

5. *Support and simplify.* Ask yourself throughout the day, "What parts of this task can be delegated, and/or how can this task be simplified or made easier?"

6. *Say no to requests that unreasonably stretch your time.* As Grove points out, "When you say yes to one thing, you are inevitably saying no to another that is perhaps more forwarding to your goals." This skill of saying no at the right time and in the right way will be developed in chapter 11.

9

Working Smarter: A Roundup of Tips, Timesavers, and Productivity Multipliers

• • •

A major Wall Street executive recently told me that he's always pleased to learn a new timesaver or efficiency tip. And *I've* learned quite a few tricks from executives. So no matter how high up the ladder you climb, helpful efficiency and timesaving ideas are always welcome. They are fun to implement, and will have a positive time-multiplying impact.

Executive Productivity Multipliers

How Three Executives Save Hours by Shaving Minutes

Great time-shavers. Dick Traum, founder and president of the New York–based Achilles Track Club, which encourages and trains disabled people to participate in races such as the New York City Marathon, is a stickler about not wasting time. Here are two of Traum's favorite timesavers:

> **1.** When possible, he schedules outside meetings first thing in the morning or late in the day, saving thereby one segment of travel because he can go straight from or to home.
>
> **2.** He tries to make lunch dates only within a block of his office.

Boost productivity by "bundling" multiple action opportunities. When sending authors on book tours, Maria Bergman, marketing coordinator for the book *Chicken Soup for the Kids' Soul,* always tries to make authors' trips even more productive by "bundling" the events with other opportunities.

HARRIED? RUSHED? THESE SERVICES CAN SAVE YOU TIME AND FRUSTRATION

You no longer have to be a rock star to hire personal services. Here are some affordable services to simplify your time and life:

Take errands and personal chores off your hands. How about calling a service to mow your lawn, walk your dog, shop for groceries—or even stand in line for you at the DMV? Schedule time-convenient house calls by beauticians, pet groomers, personal trainers. To find purveyors of these services, check out ads in local shopping papers, on supermarket bulletin boards, and local websites. Be careful to thoroughly check references before bringing anyone into your home.

Simplify your life by getting organized. Personal organizers stand ready to help you organize and coordinate both your business life and your domestic life. Visit the National Association of Professional Organizers (NAPO) at www.napo.net to find an organizer in your area.

Is "no time to cook" on your list of time burdens? Check out the U.S. Personal Chef Association. They stand ready to shop for you—then cook two weeks' worth of meals, label them, and stack them in your freezer. Want to know more? Visit www.uspca.com. These services can be pricey, but many people find them worth it for the time relief and peace of mind.

For example, she asks authors to recommend bookstores where they might schedule book signings. And she studies Yahoo! Maps for each city on the tour to locate other stores in the area where she might coordinate two signings in one day.

Fast, efficient restaurant service. Etiquette guru Letitia Baldrige suggests concentrating most of your business entertaining in one or two restaurants. You will be greeted by name, get short-notice reservations on busy days, be seated immediately, and you can arrange for your check, if you are hosting, to be added to your credit card account, so you and your guests can leave without waiting for the check.

Eight Favorite Executive Productivity Multipliers

1. SPARE MOMENTS CAN BE VERY, VERY VALUABLE TO YOU

An extremely potent productivity galvanizer is Martin Edelston's tactic of maxing out the short intervals. Edelston points out that "those spare minutes—five minutes here, ten minutes there—can be very, very valuable." Similarly, Stephen Carter, CEO of Cingular Wireless, "even if he only has ten minutes between meetings, [will] use that downtime to fire off replies and forward critical messages."

The key is to make use of the small intervals of time between meetings, in waiting rooms, or standing in line.

What you can do in five minutes:

• Scan your e-mail for the important messages.
• Set up your monthly appointment calendar.
• Start the guest list for an upcoming client reception.

What you can do in ten minutes:

• Think of ways to solve a particular problem at work.
• Compose an e-mail or memo.

- Scan a newsletter.
- Give yourself a "brain break." Sometimes the best use of time is just to look out the window and do nothing at all.

What you can do in thirty minutes:

- Skim a report, and mark the parts that need future study.
- Read journals, newspapers, and magazines that you haven't gotten to.
- Take a few bites out of a complex project. For example, if you have a speech to write for an upcoming conference, use this time to jot down some preliminary thoughts on the subject.

Ted Benavides, city manager of Dallas, Texas, says, "When I went to get my hair cut, or went to the doctor's office, I always kept a book or report in my car. I'd read Drucker's latest book" or catch up on outstanding tasks. "I'm going to be trapped there anyway—my question always was, 'What's the maximum use I can make of that time?' "

LAKEIN'S "SWISS CHEESE" STRATEGY

In *How to Get Control of Your Time and Your Life*, time-management guru Alan Lakein suggests that before "officially" beginning a big job, punch holes in it by doing small tasks whenever you can. For example, got a five-minute break between meetings? Before launching an office redecorating project, check a few Web sites for preliminary info, such as requesting catalogs from three office furniture companies. You'll punch so many holes in the project (e.g., "Swiss cheese" it), that by the time you officially sit down with it, the project will seem much less daunting.

2. JUMP-START YOUR MORNING THE NIGHT BEFORE

Start your morning the night before. You'll get out the door faster—and with less hassle—by preplanning.

Before you go to bed, put coffee in the coffeemaker . . . set out a non-perishable breakfast, such as a bowl of dry cereal . . . choose the clothes you'll wear the next day . . . and pack your briefcase and place it by the front door. Put Post-its noting any "do today" reminders, such as "pick up dry cleaning" or "get car washed," on your door, grab them as you run out the door, and put them on your dashboard as a reminder.

3. GET A JUMP ON MONDAY WITH A QUICK "BEFORE THE WEEKEND" FRIDAY REVIEW

Do a quick desk and in-box check to make sure all papers and e-mails have been TRAF'd. Put any unTRAF'd materials into your "action" file for quick dispatch on Monday.

Review your to-do list. Star your priorities for Monday, and put out on your desk the materials you'll need to launch those tasks.

Don't bypass any follow-ups from this past week that didn't get addressed. Simply reenter them digitally, or into your manual calendar, for the coming week.

Okay, you're off! Enjoy the weekend.

4. QUICK-TASK RULE

Tick any tasks on your to-do list that will take five minutes or less to accomplish. When you can, take care of them as soon as they hit your desk. But in any event, tackle at least three or four of these small tasks daily.

5. PLAN FIRST—SAVE HOURS LATER

James W. Botkin, in his book *Smart Business,* gives this advice from Dave Bogan of CFC: Follow the 15:4 rule: Spending fifteen minutes thinking about what you are going to do before you start will save four hours of wasted time later on. An individual who has thought through her workday, set priorities, and organized the day's tasks is likely to accomplish far more than someone who moves randomly through the day. So use the 15:4 rule to save time and boost efficiency for you and your staff.

6. JUMP-START WRITING PROJECTS

To jump-start preparing a report or other writing project, play writing solitaire. Jot each point you intend to develop on an index card. Then "deal them out" on your desk. Keep moving the cards around, creating different combinations until you have organized them in the way that seems most logical.

And that's your project outline.

7. CAST YOUR INFORMATION NET WIDE

Never let yourself be left high and dry because you need information from another department that you can't get. Top executives are well known throughout their careers for maintaining broad informational contacts throughout their organization and industry. For example, Terry Conrad, CEO of Merz Pharmaceuticals USA, based in Greensboro, North Carolina, makes the point that he has never lost touch with any boss he has ever worked for. Why? It's a continually useful support network, which any manager at every level can adapt.

My advice: Get to know at least two people in every relevant department, so that in whatever area you need assistance or information, there's someone available to help you out. Make it clear to these colleagues that you're always around and happy to help them.

A good way to do this is to take different routes throughout the building, creating opportunities for spontaneous interaction. Or, instead of using interoffice mail, hand-carry your stuff as an excuse to create a spontaneous conversation with someone in another department. This is a variation on MBWA, or "management by wandering around."

8. OPEN UP QUALITY TIME WITH SMALL SHIFTS IN HABITS

When we feel that we are swimming against the current and can't get anything accomplished, it's often useful in opening up quality time to make a small shift in our habits. For example, one manager, who came in every day at 7:30 a.m. to gain a "quiet hour" to work on priorities, seemed to be making little headway until he realized he was using up substantial time just pulling the relevant files and getting organized for the project he was working on. By simply shifting the preparations to the end of the previous day, in the morning he now tackles his substantive work at once—with not one minute of downtime. What a difference!

Whenever we get that "swimming against the current" feeling, we can often break free by asking a series of basic questions: "Should I do this earlier? Later?" Or, "Should I do this myself or in a team, or delegate it?" Or, "Can this process be simplified?"

Examining our routines occasionally can lead to a great new productivity booster.

ONE EXECUTIVE'S TRAVEL SMARTS

James Morris, chairman and CEO of Signator (an affiliated company of John Hancock), makes very interesting and useful comments about his own program for travel efficiency. "I do travel extensively. Currently I travel about three and a half to four business days per week. I was in Los Angeles last night, I have a dinner

(cont'd on page 124)

ONE EXECUTIVE'S TRAVEL SMARTS *(cont'd from page 123)*

in Kansas City this evening, and a dinner in Phoenix tomorrow evening. Travel time to me is no different than office time.

"One way I make travel efficient is by having 'routines' for carry-on items. You learn to adapt. And by the way, no pun intended, I carry my adapter so I don't have any downtime on the plane. My driver's license goes into my left pocket. I carry my lightweight garment bag for one-day trips and another, heavier-weight bag for longer trips, and my favorite briefcase . . .

"One thing I've learned to do to make sure I don't mislay anything is that as soon as I get on the plane I have a little routine: I put my driver's license back into my money clip; I put my briefcase on the seat; I put my garment bag in the upper compartment; and that way I'm not left wondering what I did with my driver's license, et cetera.

"I deliberately schedule conference calls during that interval while I'm waiting for a flight. [SW: That's clever.]

"I have three boxes on my desk in my office: in-box, out-box, and an 'airplane box.' My assistant, Joanne, puts everything that needs to be read and responded to—but that's not urgent—into the airplane box, for example, a sales report from the home office, or board materials to review and respond to.

"I'll take the entire contents of the airport box with me to read and work through on the plane." [SW: Also very practical.]

Team-Wise Timesavers

Today, many companies in the manufacturing, distribution, or technology areas operate with project teams. So if your working group—a departmental unit, a working team, or even a small company—

continually gets sidetracked by a series of annoying or disruptive events, then try some of these "team-wise" efficiencies and time-multipliers instituted by large companies and small.

SHORTEN TIMELINES BY ESTABLISHING TEMPLATES FOR FUNDAMENTAL PROCESSES

Executives at Johnson & Johnson were concerned because new products were taking too long to get to market. The problem was that the Food and Drug Administration kept returning J&J's new-product applications with many additional questions.

To reduce the delay, J&J captured all the previous FDA inquiries. Now, J&J's application team can anticipate FDA questions, complete the research up front, and provide answers in the initial application.

This simple initiative dramatically sped up the approval process. In one case, Johnson & Johnson made $30 million just by being able to release one product a month early.

How to adapt the template idea: A human-resources attorney who was tired of digging through the reams of material he was sent for every potential legal claim codified a checklist for the HR department that enabled them to submit to him only the key materials. He then had the option to request more detail if he needed it.

SPEED THINGS UP BY BENCHMARKING AGAINST COMPANIES OUTSIDE YOUR INDUSTRY

When Motorola wanted to trim the time between receiving orders and delivering cellular phones, it benchmarked itself against an unlikely but well-recognized fast-delivery leader: Domino's Pizza.

How to adapt the benchmarking idea: The director of employee food service for a large hospital became concerned about rising complaints about the cafeteria. He addressed the problem by consulting with the food service director of a nearby large insurance company whose in-house food service was rated highly.

FIND NEW PRODUCTS BY INSTITUTING BUYING "FORUMS"

Here's how two companies accomplished that:

Haystack Toys finds new products by sponsoring a yearly Great American Toy Hunt tour to major cities, at which toy inventors are invited to show their wares.

Henri Bendel, an ultra-exclusive Fifth Avenue specialty store, hosts a quarterly "Open See" event. Bendel's Teril Turner describes it as a "casting call" where designers of clothing, accessories, and cosmetics present their wares.

Both companies have added six new product lines a year from these open calls.

How to adapt the "expo" idea: If you are looking for a streamlined way to locate new products or services for your firm, consider developing a list of sources who might be interested in participating in an expo along the lines described above.

ARE THINGS CHANGING? HERE'S HOW HEWLETT-PACKARD EFFECTED AN EFFICIENT, ORDERLY TRANSITION

When Hewlett-Packard and Compaq merged, the "order of magnitude" of change was off the charts. Webb McKinney, who headed the integration team melding HP with Compaq, poised his team to translate integration smoothly from concept into action.

Within a couple of days after the merger's approval, HP reps visited the top 100 corporate customers of the combined company. Their mission: To present the new account teams; to show customers bound "playbooks" listing which products would continue and which would be phased out; and to offer assurances of orderly transitions to alternatives for phased-out products.

How to adapt this "orderly transition" idea: Scope out months in advance how all internal routines, systems, and individuals will be affected by the change. Be sure that all parties understand their new roles by—when appropriate—creating explanatory written materials and holding discussion and brainstorming meetings.

Two basic rules:

1. No surprises.

2. Make sure everyone knows exactly what they are supposed to do the day the change is implemented and thereafter.

KEEPING QUALITY ON TRACK

Past British Airways chairman Sir Colin Marshall, determined to build top-quality service, created a ten-member quality-control unit called the "Snoop Squad." The squad was charged with detecting flaws in BA's performance by using the airline as customers do.

The unit tracks 350 measures of performance that include on-time service, airplane cleanliness, ease of check-in, and time spent on hold when making a phone reservation.

The Snoop Squad's findings are so important that their monthly quality reports are sent to the chairman, the CFO, and other top executives.

How to adapt this quality-control idea: Create a quality-control team within your department or working unit. First, brainstorm the quality-control criteria that apply: Good lighting and responsive service in the reception area? Twenty-four-hour turnaround on calls? Better servicing for computers, printers, copiers, and other equipment? Next, design a way to capture this info. And, finally, arrange for monthly review and develop programs for improvement as necessary.

FOOLPROOF PROOFREADING

Typos and errors in important documents such as contracts and proposals can create time-consuming disasters. Perhaps your staffers can have a little fun—and still be effective—while proofreading complex documents.

Edie Jarolim, a former Wall Street law-firm proofreader, offers these tips: "We did our proofreading aloud, and in pairs, to ensure accuracy. Punctuation was specified by table taps and by enunciation. A comma was 'com,' a period 'dot,' etc. Robert, an aspiring artist . . . would sing the documents to different Broadway tunes."

How to adapt this proofreading idea: If you have ever experienced the panic caused by an error in a technical document or contract, think about training your staffers to adapt this technique.

CUT BACK ON TEAM TIMEWASTERS

One advertising company discovered that an employee was keying in the same report twice—spending six additional hours a week—because a network error didn't allow him to transfer the information to another division.

To identify the terrible timewasters in your office, hold an "efficiency evaluation" meeting with your direct reports once a quarter. To prepare, ask them (and ask them to ask *their* subordinates) to log their time for a week prior to the meeting. That will determine which tasks take up the most time. At the meeting, apply the following five questions to each major task and class of activities:

1. Is the amount of time spent reasonable and appropriate, given its benefits?
2. Are we duplicating effort?
3. Does the person responsible have the appropriate skills? Should we reassign the task or upgrade the person's skills?
4. Could we simplify it? Delegate it? Eliminate it? Can we streamline it with upgraded technology?
5. How can we reallocate any newfound time for maximum benefit?

Bill Gates made sure systems used to track consumer buying automatically highlighted "exceptions"—numbers that went outside anticipated parameters—so that managers could spend their time dealing with problem-solving instead of laboriously analyzing the numbers.

Nine More Timesaving Tips and Best Practices

1. Color-code your calendar so you can tell at a glance the status of projects or assignments. Examples: Red highlighter for high-priority items; blue for project deadlines; green for following up; black for daily scheduled work.

2. Sales or contact leads growing cold because of sluggish follow-up? With your group, create a plan of attack. Note all contacts or prospects as they occur, or gather their business cards. Every day, enter, or ask your assistant to enter, these contacts into a spreadsheet. E-mail the spreadsheet to a designated "lead coordinator," who can ship appropriate materials to the contact at once.

3. Avoid being overwhelmed with reading material. Read cooperatively. Divvy up publications among staff or colleagues, and meet monthly to have each person summarize the key items in the publications they've read.

4. Laminate some of your business cards to use as tags on your luggage, briefcase, laptop, or camera case. Besides serving as ID, they might also spark conversations that could lead to a business opportunity.

5. Do the part of the job you like least first, and then you have the good stuff ahead of you. Your own enthusiasm will give you the ideas and energy for the best part of the assignment.

6. Divide to conquer. No job looks too complex if you reduce it to a single action—which is then followed by another action. And another. Until the job is done.

7. Be sure to follow up with a thank-you note after you close a sale or for any courtesy. Leonard A. Lauder especially emphasized the importance of this courtesy. Here's an easy way to keep up-to-date on thank-you's: Keep a kit consisting of notecards and envelopes, stamps, and pens in a box that you keep next to your TV chair at home. Take a copy of every purchase order home. Then, while you're watching TV, take care of a few thank-yous. It's a simple courtesy that packs a lot of firepower.

8. Ease into a writing task that you had to break in midstream by leaving a sentence incomplete. Finishing the sentence will bring you right back into the project.

9. Use a three-ring looseleaf binder to capture all those miscellaneous advisories you don't know what to do with (fire drill instructions, infrequently used extension numbers, cafeteria hours, etc.).

Finding Your Personal Best Timestyle

Many successful executives appreciate the importance of finding their own timestyle and riding the energies, so to speak, of their own personality and temperament. In the words of Kerr-McGee's Luke Corbett, "Be yourself."

These four key elements, when put together, create a productive timestyle:

Personal jumpstarters—the things that most excite and interest you.
Strategies for relaxing and recharging your battery.
Personal prime time.
Identifying a signature "time concept."

Personal Jumpstarters: What Gets Your Juices Flowing?

Many successful executives actively seek out situations and environments that activate their mental energies.

Between laps. Peter Lewis, chairman of Progressive Insurance, gets his greatest ideas between the laps he swims. He keeps a tape recorder poised at each end of his pool to record his ideas. One pool-induced idea helped the company lower auto-insurance rates. Typically, insurers give customers estimates to take to repair shops, which encourages both customers and shops to pad the bill. Lewis's between-laps idea: Take charge of repairs and complete them at much lower cost.

"I solve most of my problems at the end of the workday, in a somewhat altered state of consciousness," Lewis says.

Structuring your brain. Marcia Zerivitz of the Jewish Museum of Florida expressed an idea that she describes as "structuring her brain." It's a way of sorting out her mental energy. For example, she'll put aside in the "tomorrow pile" a document she has to review carefully because she just isn't in the right frame of mind today, "so I don't waste my time reading it." Said Zerivitz, "I knew this could wait until tomorrow . . . so I kind of structured my brain. I'm pretty disciplined that way. I will always get to the task at the right time."

Sam Walton—energized by failure. When Wal-Mart founder Sam Walton made an error, he didn't waste time beating himself up about it. He took on something new the very next morning.

The ability to bounce back from failure is a quality every successful leader needs to perfect. It helps to think of failure as a necessary precursor to success. When you blunder, get up and try again . . . quickly.

Try this: Play back in your mind the times when you've felt most energetic and "up." Can you identify the circumstances that fostered the up feeling? Reproduce them—instituting the elements that supported your energy, and eliminating the elements that dragged you down.

BOOST PRODUCTIVITY WITH MINI-WORKOUTS

Even the busiest CEOs know that exercise can lead to better job performance.

Sunbeam CEO Jerry W. Levin admits that staying healthy is a challenge. "I need to be fit for this, because the hours are long and you are juggling so many balls at once," he says.

His advice, quoted in an article in the *Wall Street Journal:* "Don't skip your exercise because you have a meeting." Every morning he completes a series of sit-ups and stretching. He does a lightweight workout with dumbbells and he runs two or three times a week.

Kenneth Cooper's workday exercise tips

According to aerobics expert Dr. Kenneth Cooper, moderate, consistent exercise is the most underrated productivity enhancer. Here are some specific exercise tips that you can incorporate into your workday:

- Park a mile from your commuter station and walk to the train.
- Hike a quarter-mile across the parking lot rather than parking close to your building.
- Take the stairs to visit colleagues on other floors.
- Grab an exercise band or a jump rope—not a cup of coffee— when you have a spare five minutes (say, before your next meeting).
- Do some discreet isometrics at your desk or when waiting for the elevator.

Introducing exercise opportunities to your workplace

Recognizing the value of exercise to employees, many large corporations now provide in-house gyms or health clubs. If that's a bit elaborate for your firm, consider arranging for discount memberships at a nearby health club or providing small classes with a trainer. The National Music Publishers' Association in New York put a stationary bike in a small room for its employees to use.

Strategies for Relaxing and Recharging Your Battery

Take "mini-vacations" during the day. Michael Bryant, a consultant and president of Career Transition Services in Baltimore, suggests taking brief five- or ten-minute breaks during the day to help you recharge and retain your focus. Says Bryant, "Mini-breaks give you balance."

Here's how three executives take time to recharge: "I sometimes go to Expedia.com or Travelocity.com and plan an imaginary trip, like to Switzerland," says Doug Renfro, president of Renfro Foods, a family-owned salsa manufacturing business in Fort Worth, Texas. "It takes maybe five minutes, it's interesting, and it relieves stress."

Mark Porter, president and CEO of the online print service htp-print in San Francisco, calls his twenty-one-month-old daughter and "practice[s]" the alphabet with her. "Hearing her say 'Daddy' brings me back to earth if things are getting too crazy."

Sharon Keys Seal, a professional business coach in Baltimore, walks around the block. "I just started wearing a pedometer so that I can make sure I walk at least 10,000 steps a day." She also makes a midday call to her best friend in Missouri.

Retreats. Here's how Bill Gates of Microsoft and also another executive, Paul Winslow, CEO of QTI Solutions, a New Jersey–based pharmaceutical testing lab, make time to reflect.

Bill Gates would take two "think weeks" every year at his family's retreat in Hood Canal in northwest Washington to ruminate on the Next Big Thing in technology.

Paul Winslow goes to his office on New Year's Day and evaluates every outstanding project against larger goals and priorities. Projects that don't make the cut are eliminated, clearing the decks for the new year. (If a full retreat isn't in the cards for you, how about adapting this idea by devoting a few weekend hours to blue-sky thinking?)

"Administrivia" days. Consultant Jeffrey Fox finds it very relaxing to clear the decks by taking one day a month to handle all the loose ends. "Go to the library one day a month . . . Organize all your to-do projects. Knock off all the . . . 'administrivia' (those little business tasks, such as paperwork, expense accounts, report reviews, that, if not completed, can cause big problems). Organize your big projects into small, digestible pieces. Get your people file up to date . . . Write all your follow-up memos, customer letters, and thank-you notes.

"One good, uninterrupted workday in a quiet library will enable you to accomplish ten times more than you could with the same number of hours in your office."

This is a partial list of "rechargers" people have suggested as pick-me-ups. What might zing up your day?

- Take breaks during the day
- Exercise
- Listen to music
- Have a quick chat or e-mail exchange with spouse or close friend
- Read a magazine article or a chapter from a book that's not work-connected
- Take a walk
- Do yoga or meditation
- Take a ten- or fifteen-minute catnap
- Do a crossword puzzle
- Play a computer game

TAKE ADVANTAGE OF
YOUR PERSONAL PRIME TIME

Are you fresh and raring to go first thing in the morning? Or is your "high" time later in the day?

Provide a huge boost to personal productivity by making a serious effort to block out at least an hour during your prime time to handle your priorities and most demanding tasks.

Identify Your "Signature" Time Concepts

In an interesting wrinkle, some people gain productivity value by thinking of time in a characteristic way that kick-starts their energy. Here are two examples:

Staying "in the point." Tennis great Jimmy Connors said that during a match he only thinks about the point he's in. He never thinks about whether or not he's going to win. All his attention is sharpened toward what needs to be done next. When that point is completed, whether won or lost, he drops it from his mind and becomes fully absorbed in the next.

Becoming the "crisis police." One executive, who confided he is not naturally organized, described how he overcame his tendency to disorder by imposing a stronger value: creating an atmosphere of stability and calm.

"I'm consciously *not* creating a certain amount of chaos in my life. Every unreturned phone call, every dangling inquiry from a staffer or customer, every unprocessed file or e-mail is an invitation to future aggravation or crisis.

"So I think of my assistant and myself, working together, as the crisis police, catching crises before they happen through strong day-to-day organization and anticipatory planning."

10

The Multitasking Myth

• • •

A SENIOR EXECUTIVE PERSPECTIVE

In this pressured time, "multitasking"—signing documents while you're on the phone, doing ten things at once—means by definition to accomplish more and more in less and less time.

So it's a pretty safe bet that top executives are very good at multitasking. Right? Take a guess:

Most senior executives are . . .

Master multitaskers. They get more done in five minutes than most of us can in twenty-five.

Active multitaskers. They actively seek out opportunities to multitask.

Occasional multitaskers only—and that in obvious ways, such as reading reports while on a stationary bike.

That top executives were "master multitaskers" was my choice, and I was wrong. *Most senior executives do not multitask in any meaningful way.*

From time to time in this book we come upon an executive mystery: a widespread executive time-management practice that seems against expectation. This is one of those counterintuitive surprises, such as that Bill Gates, as mentioned earlier, won't even read while he's on his exercise bike, preferring to concentrate on exercising.

When do executives find multitasking appropriate, and how do they do it? And what do they do instead? When does multitasking present an actual obstacle to productivity?

Executives Don't Multitask—They "Spotlight" Task

Multitasking is one of the great time-management misunderstandings—at least so far as senior executives are concerned. In an interesting *Fast Company* piece by Alison Overholt, "The Art of Multitasking," the executives interviewed weren't, with one brief exception, actually shown multitasking at all. For example, Stephen Carter, CEO of Cingular Wireless, was shown focusing tightly on completing small tasks— dealing with e-mails in real time, processing paper memos as they showed up on his desk—but no activity was cited that would fit as multitasking.

The keys to efficiency for Marissa Peterson, executive vice-president of worldwide operations for Sun Microsystems, are planning and delegating—including to her family. Once, when a computer crash destroyed all her slides for an upcoming presentation, she made the recovery operation a family affair, assisted by her husband and two children. But multitasking also doesn't seem to be a significant part of her efficiency portfolio.

The one instance of multitasking cited in the *Fast Company* article referred to Anne Altman, an IBM managing director, who instant-messaged back and forth with a staffer while she was on the phone with a customer to obtain some updated information for the customer.

So where's the misunderstanding? Surely everyone, at every level, needs and wants to accomplish tasks efficiently within a short period of time. That goal pertains across the board. But the top executives tend to do it differently.

To visualize our way into this territory, imagine, if you will, two square objects. One artifact is a square of woven material with many crisscrossing strands. The other square is composed of many small individual pieces of mosaic tile.

Without flogging this metaphor to death, the "weave" represents a rough idea of multitasking, whereas the mosaic tiles—an image previously used in the context of TRAF—reasonably represents the concentration pattern of top executives.

Very successful executives tend, by and large, to *focus* their attention, even if very briefly, on the task or encounter immediately at hand. They are loath to diffuse attention or allow themselves to be distracted.

Yet a hallmark of this approach is that each individual turn of the kaleidoscope tends to be extremely brief. Management theorist Henry Mintzberg, in his 1973 classic *The Nature of Managerial Work,* observed that most CEO "in the corridor" encounters lasted no longer than nine minutes. I estimate that, today, most of these "spotlight" connections last no longer than three or four minutes.

But it *feels* as if the executives are multitasking, because a lot gets done in a very short period.

So what distinguishes the constant encounters of productive "spotlighting" from the daily experience some people describe as being pecked to death by ducks?

The difference is *focus.* Real "business" is happening in each brief engagement. I asked Teodoro Benavides, city manager of the city of Dallas, about my observation that senior executives don't seem to be conscious of trying to do fifty things at once.

He said, "I'm doing the most important thing when I'm doing it. I shouldn't be doing something else. I'll always have time later.

"What I'll do is, I'll write whatever new thing comes up when I'm

WHEN TO MULTITASK . . .

Laureen Ong, president of the Washington, D.C.-based National Geographic Channel, and a multitasking expert, says, in a *New York Times* article, "When you're young, you think life is eternal. But in my mid-thirties, I realized how short life was and I needed to pack more into my day. Now, I wake up at five in the morning and practice my speeches as I do back-to-back spin classes on my bike."

Another executive goes through her e-mail with her Black-Berry while walking back from lunch. Just keep an eye out for traffic! And, of course, signing purchase orders while on a conference call where your input is not needed is a classic multitasking opportunity.

Others find working out at a health club a great opportunity to multitask, checking televised stock market quotes while on the StairMaster, or reading reports while pedaling a stationary bike.

AND WHEN NOT TO . . .

But multitasking can backfire. Doing too much at once can lead to problems. For example, have you ever sent the wrong e-mail message to a client while on the phone with your boss? Also, if a staffer is filling you in on an important client meeting, you should give him or her your full attention. This isn't the time to approve invoices or sign correspondence.

concentrating on something else on a Post-it note, 'Need to think about this . . .' I'll plaster the Post-its on my desk. So when I'm driving home, listening to music full blast, is when I'll start to think, 'You know, I've got this debt service issue that I need to worry about. I need to talk to this person and that person.'

"There's always time when people aren't talking to me that I can run through this material. Then, when I come into work, I can call this person and say, 'I'm worried about this, you need to worry with me.' "

This makes "spotlighting"—which could entail 100 or more brief phone or face-to-face connections during the day (e-mail doesn't count)—a powerful personal time-management tactic. (The art of turning brief encounters into powerful engines for productivity is developed further in chapter 14.)

And twinned with spotlight focus is that bulldog-like tendency to complete projects—whether large or small.

For example, every up-the-ladder executive, having once picked up a piece of paper or opened an e-mail, wouldn't dream of not dealing with it—TRAFing it. To leave actions in a no-decision limbo—well, they are just constitutionally unable to do that.

But what about the rest of us? It'll come as no surprise that this urgent "will to completion" isn't necessarily as deeply embedded in all our genes.

What follows are some tactics to aid in developing our own ability to "spotlight focus" and to arrive at completion.

Tactics to Aid in Spotlighting

Because the drumbeat of multitasking has been so strong, many managers have suffered a reduced ability to concentrate.

Here we discuss some ways in which, instead of trying to do five things at once, you can accomplish all five of those tasks faster and more efficiently by concentrating on one task at a time.

Nancy Ratey, an ADHD coach in Wellesley, Massachusetts, offers some interesting "focusing"—spotlighting—suggestions for her clients. And you don't need to have ADHD to get value from them!

- Ask your assistant, instead of dumping a pile of notes and correspondence on your desk, to sit down with you once a day for a ten- or fifteen-minute working session. He or she hands you one file, document, or printed-out e-mail at a time. You discuss together what needs to be done, your assistant takes notes, and you both mark actions for follow-up and review. Done.

- If possible, move your direct reports' offices closer to your own, so you'll have fewer distractions on your way to talk to them.

- Make a to-do list that isn't just a million things you've got to do. Instead, highlight each day the two or three tasks that are most important.

- Color-code files for your direct reports and your major clients. Put a sticky on top of each active file listing outstanding call-backs, questions, and projects (color-coordinating stickys to match the files is even better). That way, you can tell at a glance what needs to be done.

- Start keeping a journal about your goals and intentions. Compare it two or three times a week with actions.

- Use the buddy system. Talk to a buddy for about ten minutes each morning between 7:00 and 8:00 a.m., going over the previous day's accomplishments and the goals for the coming day.

How to Boost Your Concentration

The ability to concentrate in general is high on the list of productivity strategies. Yet, in the bustle of a busy day, it's one of the hardest to accomplish. Here are some concentration tactics that will help you to, as Jimmy Connors said, "stay in the point you're in."

The Deadline Factor

Samuel Johnson famously said, "Imminent execution does concentrate the mind wonderfully." Well, it wasn't exactly execution, but Jack Welch was not amused when, after a month, his purchasing staff hadn't made much progress on an assignment he had given them. Welch promptly adjourned their meeting and directed that it reconvene in four hours with an update. His staff accomplished more in those four hours than they had in the previous month.

There can be a lot of power in the deadline factor—know your own deadline style. Do you:

- thrive under the adrenaline high of tight, tight deadlines?
- prefer to operate under moderate deadline pressure?
- tend to go blank or panic at tight deadlines?

If tight deadlines really do galvanize you, then by all means take advantage of that adrenaline high. Just don't make the mistake made by one manager who started work on an important project the night before it was due, and realized too late that he hadn't allowed time for some critical data to be sent to him.

DEADLINES AND CREATIVITY

Prominent film-score composer Elmer Bernstein (Ghostbusters, The Grifters) has this to say in a Fast Company article (July 2001) about using deadline pressure to get started:

"Generally speaking, I have learned to be a deadline worker—whether I have a deadline or not . . . If I am given all the time in the world, then I start daydreaming. There comes a moment when I have to say to myself, 'I really have to do this. Now.' That's how I trigger my creative process.

"And that reminds me of a story about Tchaikovsky. A lady asked him where he got his inspiration. And he supposedly said, 'Madam, when I walk into my studio every morning at 8:00 a.m., the muses had better be on time.'"

On the other hand, some people freeze at very tight deadlines. In that case, go the other way and build in plenty of slippage. When you estimate a project will take two weeks, add a third week.

Find the Right Setting for Concentration

This is my own concentration-enhancer: For some reason, I find it hard to concentrate on writing and thinking when I'm alone in the office, whereas I focus wonderfully well when I'm traveling. So to get that "being alone in a crowd" effect when I'm not on a train or plane, I tote my briefcase to a nearby Starbucks and become completely absorbed.

Other people, conversely, find that every little sound breaks their concentration. If you need silence, go to a conference room, close your office door, or visit the nearest public or university library.

Here's a third option: one consultant who works at home two days a week finds that every bird chirp throws him off. So he keeps the radio and TV going to create "white noise."

Five More Concentration Tips

1. Start thinking of your work in terms of results instead of activities. Example: Don't say to yourself, "I'll work on these reports for one hour." Instead, say, "I'll finish ten reports before going to lunch." That way, you concentrate on completing the work rather than watching the clock.

2. Keep a daily "action diary." According to Michelle Durst, a vice-president of human resources at Merrill Lynch, in a *Fast Company* article (April–May 1998), "Keeping track of what you do is much more important than I'd expected . . . I started a daily diary of my work. It helps my manager, and it keeps me focused from day to day and from week to week."

3. Work standing up to concentrate and avoid procrastination. Create a chest-high workspace where you can read and riffle through paperwork. If you need to make routine phone calls, make them standing up. This will lead to shorter, more focused conversations.

4. On routine assignments, watch the clock. Keep checking the time as you complete routine assignments. This visual reminder can prod you to work faster.

5. Create contests with yourself. Set a timer for ten minutes and try to complete a task before the buzzer sounds. Don't rush so much that you make mistakes, but impose a realistic time limit to turn drudgework into fun.

11

Managing Multiple Priorities

. . .

Peter Drucker has pointed out that while successful managers vary widely in temperament, interests, and even ability, they have one thing in common: a talent for getting the right things done. That means having the courage and foresight to concentrate on critical tasks, rather than trying to do it all. It means, to a degree, practicing a form of triage in the workplace each day, always making critical decisions about what needs to be done *now* and what can wait until later.

Does the way you spend your time reflect your priorities?

Or, no matter how hard you try, do you have that sinking feeling that you're never going to get to that really critical project?

The answer to your dilemma can be complex, because senior executives exercise two sets of priorities: First, the critical "must-do's" that most of us think of when we assess our priority tasks. For example, let's say you're in charge of getting an industry trade show exhibit up and running in two weeks. That is a time-sensitive priority you rank as urgent.

But then there are the subtler and more complex underlying strategic priorities that basically determine not whether the ship's brass is polished and the boilers are stoked, but whether the ship is going in the right direction.

For example, say you're a manager in a traditional department store. You are facing stiff competition from a local Target, which is attracting a worrisome portion of your upscale customer base. You have some ideas about developing a proposal to senior management about ways to protect your market share to counteract this threat.

Since the two kinds of priorities appear on the surface to be dissimilar, we'll separate tactical priorities from strategic ones, and then at the end of this chapter show how they are inexorably linked.

Tactical Priorities: Managing Multiple Must-Do's

Setting Realistic Priorities and Best Practices
One executive said to me, "I just figure out what the priorities are and execute them." Nice job. But sometimes figuring them out isn't such

You might want to try this structured "priority" to-do list designed by consultant Linda Cassell Jones.

A STRUCTURED TO-DO LIST

Major Projects	Other Business Tasks	Personal and Pleasure	Special Projects
The number-one priority tasks ... what you're most concerned about.	The regular number-two medium-priority tasks of your day.	Who do I want to have lunch with?	If, for example, you're in charge of office renovation, then tasks connected with that project go here.

Here's a good idea: Prepare your list each Friday, and update it during the week. Your priorities will always be ready when you are.

an easy task. Where to start? The answer is that you must get a fix on your priorities every day. One way to get started: organize your to-do list daily per the chart on page 148.

Many executives follow this three-part method to stay on top of the must-do's:

1. Keep your priority list at the ready. When things get hectic, priority lists easily tend to get buried on your desk. This can create havoc. Selecting from these tips will help you to locate your priorities at a glance.

- Keep your priority list or PDA at a fixed spot on your desk, or tucked into your calendar, so you always know where it is.
- Use distinctively colored paper that will always show up regardless of the pile-up on your desk.
- Attach a yellow priority sticky to your PC monitor, or tape your list to the bookshelf or wall behind your PC.
- Highlight your priorities with stars or in red—whatever gets your attention.

2. Delegate, delegate, delegate. Virtually every top executive has honed to a fine art the instinct to delegate. It's as basic as breathing. Their mantra is, *If someone else can take on a task or responsibility, or can be trained to do so, then it should by definition be delegated.*

Beth Hanson, client relationship manager at Forum Financial Group in Portland, Maine, stays on top of her workload by continually asking herself, "Is this task my highest and best use?" If not, she passes it to a staffer. (If you don't have staff, see the section on delegation in chapter 14, page 223, which describes how to delegate when you don't have anyone to delegate to.)

3. When Do You Do What? Let Your Prime Time Be Your Guide. A daily quiet hour when you're at your personal best to work solely

ORGANIZE YOUR TO-DO LIST TO REFLECT
PRIORITY INTENSITY

To sort out what's important, organize your daily to-do list according to priority intensity:

1. Top priorities	time-based "must-do's" tasks that require you to be at your sharpest tasks that are stressful or unpleasant
2. Medium priorities	medium-level tasks of the day
3. Infrastructure priorities	basic TRAF catching up on phone calls, reading, etc.
High-payoff priorities	Tasks in which the outcome is uncertain, but, if successful, can result in a career breakthrough. Maybe you're an accountant who desires to become more visible in your field. Publishing a paper for an industry journal could boost your professional standing. This is a high-payoff priority. So try to accomplish a high-payoff priority task—or part of a task, such as writing the outline of your paper—at least twice a week. If necessary, make an appointment with yourself and schedule it on your calendar!
Negative priorities	Tasks with negative consequences if you *don't* accomplish them. For example, if a key client's phone call is not returned, even if it is not particularly important in itself, then the client might get annoyed, which could lead to a relationship that spirals into negative territory.

on top priorities is absolutely ESSENTIAL to maintaining priority control. See chapter 8 for strategies on how to claim your priority time. Assign number-one priorities to your priority hour. Intersperse number-two or medium priorities throughout the day, and save your number-three tasks for the time of day when you're dragging—for most people, late afternoon.

Urgent Versus Important

The distinction we are all aware of between "urgent" and "important"—first delineated by R. Alec Mackenzie in his 1972 classic *The Time Trap* and then later by Stephen R. Covey in *The 7 Habits of Highly Effective People*—is extremely valuable in sorting out tasks that cry out from those that are less clamorous.

Yes, you've got to prepare that client presentation for next Thursday. But equally important, though less clamorous, is ensuring that you and your team all agree on the basic thrust of the presentation. Squabbling in front of the client is unprofessional and can have disastrous consequences.

DON'T AVOID TACKLING THE PAINFUL PRIORITIES

James Morris, chairman and CEO of Signator, suggested that perhaps the most important priorities message is, "Don't prioritize your day based on what's easiest and least painful. You have to prioritize on the basis of the importance of the task . . . You need to tackle the critical 'needs to be done.'

"Too many people prioritize based on their pain threshold. They get to things lower on the importance scale. For example, they'll foot-drag returning the call of a broker/dealer who is not happy with you."

Eleven Ways to Say No to Other People's Priorities
Without Making Them Angry

There are almost always many more activities on the table than time available to accomplish them. So a key skill in focusing on the tasks and projects that best showcase your strengths and give you the greatest return on your time investment is to judiciously exercise the "no" button. Developing this habit will give you the time you need to pursue your own priorities and conserve precious energy.

One thing you will quickly realize is that your colleagues will appreciate "no" much more than you might think. As a sales director in a major book publishing company once said: "No is an answer. Thank you for the clear direction." Indecision is a terrible thing in a business. Giving a clear and direct answer, in a timely way, works to the advantage of everyone.

Laurel Cutler, when she was vice-chairman of the ad agency FCB/Leber Katz, said, "The path of my life and career has been learning to say no. Perhaps taking 'No' lessons is the real key to time management." Here are a few ways of "getting to No":

GO THE DIRECT ROUTE

- *Just say "I'm going to have to say no."* A simple, direct refusal can save you—and your colleagues—a bundle of time and energy. Add "my other commitments won't allow me to," or "I'm sorry, I've made a promise to myself to focus on my three top projects this month."

- *Sandwich "no" between two affirmative statements.* For example, "I admire what you're doing. I'm not able to help, but I wish you well."

TRY SAYING "NO" WITHOUT USING THE WORD

- *Substitute the word "however."* "I appreciate your idea. However, the overtime it would require would quickly put us over budget."

- *Explain which activities you'd have to eliminate to meet the request.* "I'd like to help plan the conference, but I'd have to cancel my new client meeting in Denver."

FUDGE IT

- *Say "let me check with my manager."* Then get back later and say, "She's got a priority project that has to go to the front of the line."

SUGGEST AN ALTERNATIVE

- *"I can't do it,* but perhaps you can speak with Marion. She's a real expert on the subject."

PROPOSE A COMPROMISE OR POSTPONE

- *Compromise.* "I can't join your team, but I can devote an hour a month to lend a hand."
- *Scale down the commitment.* "I can't help you write the speech, but I'd be glad to listen to it and give you feedback."
- *Postpone.* "If my current project moves along quickly, I may be able to jump in and help. Check back with me next Wednesday."

HANDLING THE BOSS

- *When your boss asks you to take on more work,* show him or her all the projects you're currently working on. Ask which one should take priority.
- *If you have an important engagement* on a night you're unexpectedly asked to work late, offer to come in early the next morning to do the task instead.

HOW ONE STRESSED MANAGER
INVENTED A WORKABLE PRIORITY SYSTEM

"I've never been very good at setting priorities," says Tim Chamberlain, managing partner of Beverly Interiors, a $1-million full-service interior design firm in Dallas. When his business took off overnight, he realized, "I had to change or the business would sink."

Chamberlain had been spending huge blocks of time jotting down everything he had to accomplish that day, which meant that most mornings a seven-page to-do list greeted him, left over from the previous day. He even fielded frantic phone calls during dinners. "I was on the clock twenty-four hours a day. I tried every kind of calendar and none worked for me," he said. "I felt so beat up. There was no downtime with friends, no time for any personal life."

So, several years ago, Chamberlain devised his own system.

Tim Chamberlain's ingenious Post-it priority system

- *Focus on priorities.* Chamberlain writes two mission statements—one professional, one personal—to clarify what is important. He revises these statements periodically, and carries both with him every day. In part, the missions state: "My goal is to provide an outstanding level of service to my clients, maintain meaningful relationships with my friends, and give substantially to the community of both my time and resources."
- *Set a weekly agenda.* Setting a weekly agenda gives Chamberlain a bigger picture, and thus a better grasp of what he needs to get done. "Knowing my priorities makes it easier to say no when I have to."
- *Execute your priorities.* Chamberlain uses a flexible, color-coded, client-based to-do list organized around his calendar.

He writes every task or deadline on an individual Post-it note and sticks it on a weekly calendar he can place on his desk and carry in his briefcase. The Post-its are color-coordinated to match each client's color-coded folder, so he can quickly see which client items need attention on any given day.

Instead of crossing out and rewriting his to-do list, Chamberlain just moves his Post-its around. "It's not as daunting to look at," he explains. "And it's more flexible, too." (Your Company—Forecast 1997)

More Priority-Handling Wisdom from Executives

This roundup of executive priority-handling nuggets is gathered from executives' years of experience:

Give your day a sharp focus. Joy Soto Kocar, a technical writer in California, says, in *The HP Palmtop Paper,* "Before I even turn on my computer, I review my to-do list and ask myself these two questions: What are the most *important* to-do's for me to handle today? And which to-do's will help me *clear the decks* for a successful day—for example, cleaning out my call list? Asking myself both of these questions at the start of each day helps me focus on important priorities and makes my time most productive."

One time-pressured head of a major U.S. firm keeps adding to his to-do list through the course of the day—phone calls to make, memos to write, ideas to follow up on. At the end of each workday he dictates his list, specifying due dates and order of priority to his assistant. His assistant types up his priority list and puts it on his desk each morning. Longer-range tasks are entered into a tickler file and then added to the typed to-do list for that day.

Here's another executive idea: List your priorities and goals on a pocket-sized card for a convenient and instant reminder of what is most important to you. When someone asks for your time, consult the card and ask yourself, "Will this meeting further any of my goals?"

Align your priorities with your manager's priorities. Never work at cross-purposes with your manager. It's a sure-fire prescription for wheel-spinning and frustration. Said one executive, "I made it a practice to sit down with my manager once a quarter to compare what *I* thought my priorities were with his idea of my priorities."

The "don't-do" list. Galvanize your ability to focus on top priorities by creating a "don't-do" list: What *shouldn't* I be spending my time on?

Mary Rudie Barneby, of UBS Financial Services, Inc., said, "I've really learned to be smart about what I don't do anymore, and that to me has been the secret to my success."

As consultant Sandra Kresch suggests, "If you focus your attention on the five things that you must absolutely get accomplished, as opposed to the fifteen things that one doesn't absolutely have to focus on, then I think you have a better shot at getting it done."

When You Need to Let Priorities Shift

Nothing throws people more than when previously agreed-upon priorities are upended, such as when you arrive in the office with your game plan ready to execute and your priorities for the day all set, only to have your manager pop in and tell you to drop everything—his boss needs a report by 3:00 p.m.

It is truly distressing. And to add insult to injury, your previous priorities don't usually disappear when new ones come along—it's just new priorities on top of the old. But having to shift priority gears goes with the territory. As circumstances change, you have to change with them. So how do you deal with this inevitable frustration when it occurs?

Here's where senior executives have a lot to teach us, for with being at the top seems to come an attitude of flexibility and an acceptance of change.

First, and very important: Align your interest with your manager's. No eye-rolling, no expletives. Consult with him or her about how best to tackle the tasks that are being put aside. Can they be delayed or handed off? Or do you just have to bite the bullet and do them all?

The priority here is to establish a consultative relationship to support your manager, and therefore support your team.

Second, try to anticipate your manager's changing priorities. Make sure to have a weekly touch-base with your boss, even a couple of minutes on the fly, to ask, "Is anything coming up that we should talk about?" This question is likely to elicit information that your boss might otherwise forget to tell you that might force an upcoming change in plans.

Also consider this systematic weekly review that Donald Guinn, well before he became head of Pacific Telesis, undertook weekly, according to a 1988 *Fortune* article. He developed the custom of reviewing on Sunday evenings everything he had done during the previous week. Before laying aside the past week's agenda, Guinn asked himself, "Why did I do all these things?"

The resulting answers and insights often led to changes in priorities and in the way he handled his time. As Guinn said, "There is no point in trying to manage your time unless you are willing to change the way you spend it."

So follow Guinn's lead and try to anticipate by asking yourself at least weekly, "Has something happened that might cause my priorities to shift?" As Karen Horn, managing director of Marsh Private Client Services, a subsidiary of Marsh & McLennan, pointed out when a bill had been passed in Congress that changed longtime banking rules, "There is no question but that we need to spend a significant portion of time thinking about the implications for our industry and our organization."

Test the winds of change. Consider the implications both in your own immediate work life and in the larger picture of anticipated or actual changes. For example, say your company has announced an attrition policy. Okay, there won't be immediate layoffs, but as people get promoted or leave, your staff resources will diminish. A priority task is to plan for that right now.

Also, in a very positive key, Faye Davis, corporate vice-president of facilities at Sprint, makes an excellent point about people needing to rethink their priorities as they move to new jobs: "When people move to the next level, they need to reconceive their jobs. They need to ask their boss or one of their peers, 'What do you see as changed in priorities [in terms of how I spend my time]? What do you see as different about this job?' "

She added, "Seek counsel—recognizing that there *is* a change in responsibility in the new job. When you get promoted to a new job, [you have to have a different perspective on your responsibilities]. Otherwise, you haven't promoted *yourself.*" And remember, when you get a new job or a promotion, people expect you to ask basic and general questions. It's easy in the first six months or so, but gets harder as time goes by and people expect you to know what you're doing.

THE PRIORITY TASK ACCOMPLISHMENT MULTIPLIER EFFECT

Successfully completing some number of tasks—large and small—every day, every week, and every month has a tangible psychological payoff. You feel better because you've accomplished something, and that positive feedback enables you to work harder, better, and more economically. It's a self-propelling cycle of accomplishment and reward that offers you a great psychological and professional benefit.

During my studies of the organization and time-management strategies of CEOs, I found that, like all of us, they all wring every ounce of value they can out of these priority nuggets. At the same time I discovered that, as with interruptions, discussed in chapter 13, senior executives are also governed by a more complex mental process when it comes to strategic priorities.

In the following section of this chapter, I will strive to clearly explain the processes they employ, so you can use them to the extent that seems fitting at this juncture in your career. As you'll soon see, this question of managing *strategic* priorities has to do with the priorities that can ultimately make or break a career or company.

Strategic Priorities: Focusing on the Right Things

At the start of this chapter I asked, "Does the way you spend your time reflect your priorities?" We then zeroed in on best practices to accomplish your tactical priorities. Now we turn to the strategic priorities— more akin to the roadmap that sets you in the right direction. Though more abstract and subliminal, they are critical to ensuring that your ship stays on the right course.

As one senior executive observed, "The majority of managers get overwhelmed by the minutiae of their job. They can't see the big picture. Therefore they can't manage their time because they can't focus on the key items."

But what are the key items? Back when Donald Guinn headed Pacific Telesis in the 1980s, he distinguished between the two dimensions of managing his time: "tactical" and "strategic."

"You could participate in efficient meetings and therefore make a good tactical use of your time," Guinn said. "But should you have participated in the meeting in the first place? Should the meeting even have been held? That's when it becomes strategic."

Often the distinction between tactical and strategic priorities is not compellingly obvious because you may not have framed your overall objectives in concrete terms. So in this section of the chapter, I topline the three basic types of "directional" priorities CEOs utilize to achieve their long-term goals, and give examples from leading executives.

Then we turn to practical approaches based on these concepts to help you determine your own strategic priorities.

The Three "Directional" Priorities

Executives guide their behavior and regulate their time choices according to central guiding principles they have defined as critical. There are three primary directional priorities:

> direct payback
> key agendas
> objective-driven

THE "DIRECT PAYBACK" PRIORITY

Both Jack Gallaway and Gerry Roche made the point that their priorities relate directly to revenues—to the heart of the business. Said Gallaway, who is now president and COO of Isle of Capri Casinos, in his former capacity of general manager of the Tropicana Hotel in Atlantic City: "The number-two guy in the hotel is the EVP of Casino Operations. He controls hundreds of millions of dollars of revenue. My door's open to him anytime. I would just leave a meeting if there was a problem and he needed to see me . . . Measured against the centrality of the business or the core of the business, this person or issue is a priority."

Roche made a similar point, and then gave it an additional resonance. He said, "I have a list of candidates for top jobs I'm currently carrying—and those candidates are my product, for which I'm invoicing my client. So that's the top priority. Then it's great to do the nice things. I call them 'WIBNIs': 'Wouldn't it be nice if . . .' So I'm sitting down with you writing a book, or recently I went out on a

KEEPING YOUR EYE ON THE PRIZE

Norman Rentrop, CEO of the German publishing house Rentrop Verlag, has a nifty way to ensure that he never forgets his key agenda: He posts his key agenda priority—boosting sales by 20 percent, for example—on a sign on the inside of his office door, next to his coat hook. When he hangs up his coat in the morning, the sign prompts him to ask himself, "What will I do today to reach this goal?" And when he puts on his coat at the end of the day, the sign reminds him to ask, "What have I done today to accomplish this goal?"

These regular prompts keep him pointed toward his goal—and prevent the hubbub of day-to-day work from pushing it aside.

friend's boat for the day . . . That's fine if my commitments are under control. But I have to live up to my commitments . . . I reevaluate my time constantly to make sure my commitments are under control. And if I seem to be getting too close to that line, I'll ask my AA to reschedule or cancel some of the WIBNIs."

Gallaway and Roche described a powerful concept: a kind of pole star that lights the way to show how priorities should be ordered, according to how close or far away they are from the business core. Though you may not be responsible for revenue intake, this idea of placing a "core concept" with a direct payback at front and center is an intriguing and powerful one. To give you an idea of how you can employ it at any level, here are two more examples of direct-payback priorities, one related to revenues, one to the goal of improving patient care.

More effective sales efforts by staff. Janet Isenberg, director of business development at New York–based Find/SVP, defined as a priority taking an hour a day to rewrite the company's sales manual. A huge project, lasting a month or two.

The direct payback? More-effective sales efforts by her staff, which would yield new business and profit.

Better patient care. Many hospital emergency rooms were becoming clogged to the point of paralysis with non-urgent cases that were not being treated because of urgent-case care. Many ERs have created a non-urgent "fast track" by dedicating one doctor to handle only simple cases.

The direct payback? Separating noncritical patients cut their wait almost in half without delaying urgent-case care, allowing other ER personnel to focus their energies on the truly critical cases.

Here's a scenario most managers can identify with that shows how you can organize your efforts around a strategic priority based on direct payback: In lean and mean corporate environments, chances are that senior leadership has issued directives to reduce overhead by a certain percentage—let's say 15 percent.

Your goal, as head of customer service, is to avoid any reduction in quality or productivity while maintaining morale. So, working off this 15 percent directive as a strategic priority, your practical task becomes to devote 15 percent of your time over the next three months to develop tactics that will enable you to cut labor costs while maintaining 24/7 customer service—perhaps a flexible job-sharing plan, perhaps developing a brainstorming program among your group to jump-start new ideas.

THE "KEY AGENDAS" PRIORITY

The notion of priorities based on one, two, or three underlying dominant agendas or themes brings us squarely into the territory of CEOs and super-successful executives. A key agenda is a theme, a powerful idea, part of the executive's personal belief system that informs, and in many respects dominates, his or her time allocations over the day, week, and year.

Here is a powerful example: L.A. police chief Bill Bratton, previously

Identify a core goal with a direct payback such as increasing revenues or maximizing sales efforts. This can serve as a touchstone around which to organize daily or weekly priority tasks. Then try one of these tacks:

- *"Dedicated" time.* Choose five hours over the course of the week—put them on your calendar—to tackle a core goal.
- *Shift to the "staff track."* Ask a staffer or intern to reorganize confused project files or to plow through backed-up reading and highlight the important points.

You will never "have time." Committing resources to completing direct-payback tasks is the only way to reach your goal.

New York City's "top cop," lives by one basic theme that guides and informs his sense of what his job really is: "Lower disorder and fear."

Sounds vague, perhaps. But part of the art of the senior executive is the ability to translate a powerful governing concept into personal day-to-day priorities.

For instance, when Bratton was New York City police commissioner under Rudy Giuliani, operating off this key agenda, he spent an enormous amount of personal time supervising the development of COMPSTAT, a sophisticated, computer-based, real-time statistical system that tracked on a daily basis all crimes committed in New York City.

With COMPSTAT, "hot spots" could be instantly identified, vulnerable precincts would show up on the system—all could be determined on a current basis and corrective action taken at once. Many people attribute the dramatic drop in the city's crime rate in part to the "instant response" capabilities made possible by COMPSTAT.

To Bratton, this capacity for instant response and the notion that the police should be held accountable for their day-to-day effectiveness were key elements in lowering disorder and fear. So COMPSTAT took pride of place as one of Bill Bratton's key personal priorities.

Bratton's example shows how developing a key agenda can have an enormous impact on how you manage your time.

John Tepper Marlin, chief economist in the New York City comptroller's office, told me that he found Bratton's key agenda, lowering disorder and fear, an extremely powerful concept. Tepper Marlin said that after learning about it, he developed a key agenda in his own realm. He feels it is now a powerful motivator and guide to his priorities on a broad day-to-day basis.

Here are more examples, from Jack Welch, Lee Iacocca, and other executives, of personal priorities that are framed by a governing idea,

VERNA GIBSON'S PRIORITY PROGRAM:
TRY TO KEEP EVERYONE CENTRALLY FOCUSED
ON THE MOST IMPORTANT THING TO DO

First, view the opportunities—what is the most central thing?
Next, get the horses in place—the resources that are necessary to achieve it.
Finally, put the disciplines in place that are necessary to achieve it.

along with ideas on how you can springboard from their example to develop your own key agendas:

Cultivating people. Jack Welch spent more than 50 percent of his time spotting talented executives and giving them assignments to grow their capabilities. He committed time each month to the GE Management Training Center at Crotonville, New York, for this express reason.

Let's say one of *your* agendas is "cultivating good people." You're working on a report evaluating the effect of international currency fluctuations on your division's Asian market, and you ask one of your colleagues, who has spent time working for a bank in Indonesia, to brainstorm with you on this topic. This could not only be helpful to you, but could enlarge your own sophistication about currency fluctuation. And if you and your colleague work compatibly, perhaps you will be a resource for each other in the future.

Not every venture will pay off so immediately. But the multiplier effect of frequently applying your key agenda to day-to-day activities is real. Remember what we learned in chapter 9 about wandering the halls, delivering your own interoffice mail, and creating opportunities to have informal, spontaneous interaction with people. This is a hallmark strategy of senior leadership in American business.

Influencing others and conveying messages to them. Lee Iacocca made it his business each year to attend the auto dealers' show, even if he had other pressing business, to define the dealer relationship as a priority.

If a key agenda is influencing others and conveying messages to them, here's how that might translate into action: When customer complaints start abruptly spiking, you decide to show up at the monthly customer service meeting—which you don't usually do. Your mere presence signals your interest in what the group is doing to correct the problem, and that getting to the bottom of this is vital.

Creating a "philosophy of relationship." To Brian Kurtz, executive vice-president of Boardroom, Inc., the web of communication is itself a priority. Says Kurtz, "Every phone call that comes in on my phone gets returned—usually by me. Even sales calls are returned. There is a definite message to the caller that your call is valued."

To Kurtz, being faithfully responsive is intertwined with an attitude that expresses value and regard in a context that could open up new business connections and opportunities.

If you are cultivating a "philosophy of relationship," you might begin by seeking out opportunities to get involved in industry associations. Another outlet is to volunteer for activities that could both serve the community and begin a web of relationships—perhaps with executives of your company—through shared volunteer activities.

Maximizing the strength of your sales force. In the section on the direct-payback priority, we saw how Janet Isenberg wanted to create a new sales manual for the sales force.

That priority task was the likely fruit of an underlying "key agenda" priority, i.e., maximizing the strength of your sales force.

A natural progression, after the new manual is completed, might be to invest in additional training; to upgrade technology to reduce response time; and to establish a monthly book group to discuss and implement ideas from sales classics.

As you can see, a "key agenda" priority can galvanize motivation to accomplish a host of projects that will help you achieve your goal.

THE "OBJECTIVE-DRIVEN" PRIORITY

This category tends to be very specific, measurable, and often time-sensitive. Almost every manager at every level has a priority that fits these criteria.

For example, when Carly Fiorina became CEO of Hewlett-Packard in 1999, two of her priority objectives were to consolidate operations and to consolidate dealings with H-P's 100 top customers so they could be serviced by one group. To accomplish the former, Fiorina telescoped H-P's former eighty-three businesses into only twelve: "Front-end" groups targeting customer activities such as marketing and sales, and "back-end" groups tackling internal activities such as producing computer and printer products. To bring about the latter objective, Fiorina dubbed Ann Livermore, who organized the consolidation, "Ann Amazon, warrior woman," to celebrate a large "cross-company" deal Livermore put together with Amazon.com.

The Priority Quadrant

PRIORITIES COME IN FOUR FLAVORS.
CATEGORIZE THE CURRENT PRIORITIES ON YOUR TO-DO LIST
BY PLACING EACH ITEM IN ONE OF THE QUADRANTS

TASK-BASED	THEME-BASED
Quadrant 1	**Quadrant 3**
"Must-do's," often with specific deadlines	"Key agenda" priorities
EXAMPLE: A report due next Thursday.	EXAMPLES: Cultivating and bringing on people, maximizing the strength of the sales force, influencing.
My list:	My list:
1.	1.
2.	2.
3.	3.
Quadrant 2	**Quadrant 4**
Direct payback priorities	Objective-driven priorities
EXAMPLE: A task or time allocation directly related to revenues or other specific business vectors.	EXAMPLES: Consolidating operations, reducing overhead.
My list:	My list:
1.	1.
2.	2.
3.	3.

The difference between objective-driven priorities and key agendas is that objective-driven priorities generally target a specific outcome, and then end, except for periodic reviews, whereas key agendas can continue to inform priority choices for years or, as in the case of Jack Welch, throughout an entire career.

In your work you may not have such complex and sophisticated long-term goals, but consider adapting these methods by seeking opportunities to apply their spirit of focus and prioritization to your own work.

To actualize agendas and objectives from Quadrants 3 and 4, you must translate them into Quadrant 1 and 2 tasks. This can seem complicated until you realize what a "crossroads" concept the notion of priorities really is.

A New Method of Translating Priorities into Accomplishment

The word *priorities* usually conjures up images of Quadrant 1 tasks. I've never seen priorities sorted out in this thematic fashion before. Your decision whether to draw from the full range of priorities to create your personal priority program, or to stick pretty much within Quadrant 1, is more than a time-management choice. It's a valid career choice.

There are lots of good reasons to choose to live your work life within the first quadrant. Perhaps your personal galvanizing agenda is non-business-related. You're a solid and conscientious worker, but your heart is with your family, civic or charitable commitments, or a personal passion such as sailing or collecting antiques. Your work is, to a large extent, a way to finance the rest of your life. Or perhaps you love exactly what you're doing and have no desire to change. For instance, there's a well-known book editor who possesses a strong track record in seeking out serious books, working closely with the authors to sculpt them, and launching the books successfully.

Although she's been approached many times on the strength of her track record to move into a management position, she has consistently refused, telling friends, "My company would lose a good editor and gain a terrible executive. Meanwhile, I'd make more money and be miserable. Where's the sense in it?"

On the other hand, if you're a professional who seeks some degree of "breakout" in your career, you will benefit from learning how to integrate all four priority quadrants in a way that generates productivity and enhances your image internally.

For those of you in the latter category, picture a framework to hold it all together—the "priority compass."

The Priority Compass—When Priorities Compete

How do you know how to allocate your time when priorities compete? Leila, a manager in the insurance industry, presented this problem:

"My department is responsible for the 'care and feeding' of our largest corporate clients. I was invited to a meeting the other day to discuss some important client issues that had come up. At the same time, my boss had assigned me the task of developing an upgraded training program for our client service representatives—the people who actually do most of the interacting with our clients. Too many questions were being kicked up to higher-ups because our service reps didn't seem to know how to handle them. Because both the meeting and the training program are real priorities, I couldn't figure out which activity was the best use of my time."

What I believe senior executives do, somewhat instinctively, when faced with competing priorities, is to organize their choices around an internalized "priority compass."

HOW TO USE THE COMPASS GUIDE TO PRIORITIES:

Here is a simple diagram of a priority compass (feel free to make copies for your own use).

I asked the insurance executive, Leila, to write in at each cardinal point of the compass (N, S, E, W) a priority theme or broad objective—

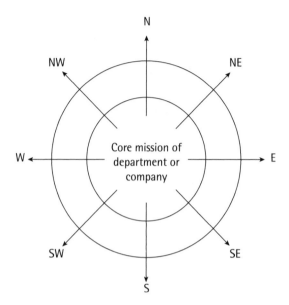

that is, her "directions" (Quadrants 3 and 4)—and also to write in the center the core mission of her department.

She said the core mission of the department was "maximum service to client." Two of her own priority themes were "to be a genuine support to my manager" and "better life/work balance" (her other two directions don't apply to this discussion).

With "support my manager" as one of Leila's main themes, then the choice between the meeting and the training program became clear. Carrying on with the training program directly supported her boss. The meeting, on the other hand, though important, didn't relate directly to any of her basic "directions."

So—always, always, always the first question—Leila asked herself, "Is there anyone who could help me with this?" She immediately thought of her direct report, Neil, and asked him to go to the meeting as her representative, with the mandate to report back to her on decisions reached and the "vibes"—or general mood—that predominated in the room.

This compass idea is not fixed or immutable. For example, political factors might have made it unwise to send a subordinate to a meeting to which she was invited—though in this case that didn't apply.

But the compass does give you a way to structure and sort out priorities. Sometimes, if "support your manager" is North and "connect to the family" is East, you have to go Northeast.

Leila wanted to get home early on Thursday in time for her daughter's championship soccer game, while still supporting her boss with the training project.

So on Wednesday night she arranged to stay in town at a friend's home so she could get to the office at 6:00 a.m. on Thursday, which gave her time to finish her preparation of the first draft of the training program before she left the office at 4:00 p.m. to get to her daughter's game.

Trading Up: Along the Arc of Executive Possibility

What If You Had an Extra Hour a Day?
HOW YOU CAN RAISE THE ANTE BY INCORPORATING KEY AGENDAS AND OBJECTIVES INTO YOUR OWN TIME PROGRAM

To enter, probably more deeply than in any other exercise in this book, into the CEO attitude or mindset, and to increase your own value to your working community, explore this exercise either in whole or in part:

1. Write down one, two, or three (but no more) governing themes and/or objectives à la Bratton, Welch, and Fiorina. Feel free to adapt one or more of the themes discussed in this section, or choose your own. If themes don't spring to mind, ask yourself, "If I had an extra hour, what would I do?"

The first tasks that spring to mind very likely embody the germs of your themes. For example, "I'd update the sales manual" might soon crystallize into "maximize the strength of our sales force."

2. Constantly, at least six times a day, think of ways to incorporate your theme into your daily tasks and Quadrant 1 priorities. (If you've chosen more than one theme, alternate them each day.) For example, the currency guy asked himself, "Who could help me with this project?" and made a valuable new connection with his colleague.

3. Once you've become accustomed to connecting your themes with your ordinary tasks, you might start gradually introducing specific, theme-related tasks as was described in connection with the seeker after the web of connection (page 163).

4. At this point you could begin aggressively developing programs connected with your themes as described on page 164 in connection with "maximizing the strength of your sales force."

Undertaking this exercise, even in a modest way, will unlock the door to many new possibilities—and thematic "priority setting" is exciting!

Simply becoming aware of this way of operating, even if you do not choose it for yourself, can only enlarge your horizon.

12

Meetings That Work

• • •

A PRIME SENIOR EXECUTIVE TOOL

It's probably safe to say that 99 percent of managers in business today view many meetings as colossal timewasters. It's absolutely counterintuitive, therefore, to see meetings—defined in the context of this chapter as scheduled, calendared events such as weekly staff meetings—as a time-management asset instead of a liability.

I'm guessing that your own instinctive take on meetings is that they steal valuable and often precious time away from your day that you need to get vital tasks accomplished. But in studying the time-management habits of CEOs and super-successful executives, I've discovered some interesting things about the real value of meetings.

I started by conducting an informal poll of colleagues and clients and asked, "What is your greatest timewaster?" It was no surprise to me that after "interruptions" came "meetings"—dull meetings, excessive meetings, too-long meetings. Management guru Peter F. Drucker has even called meetings "a concession to deficient organization."

But here's the executive paradox: Pose that same question to successful CEOs and high-level executives, and you get a surprisingly different answer. Not one top executive I interviewed said that meetings per se were a waste of time.

In a 1990 *Fortune* article, Andrew Grove, former chairman of Intel, said that "meetings provide an occasion for managerial activities. Meetings are the essential medium of managerial work. Saying they're the biggest waste of time in business is like saying the canvas is the biggest waste of time to a painter—because he stands in front of it all day."

I think this difference of opinion about meetings can be resolved by an insight shared by Gaston Caperton, head of the College Board, about the two basic kinds of meetings that exist in the business world:

One kind of meeting is fairly strictly defined. It's about managing the plan, discussing where you are based on what you said you were going to do. The other kind of meeting is more free-form. The point is to develop ideas about a project or a program or a plan. This is a meeting that encourages the play of ideas, brainstorming, and getting people's points of view.

The key is that you need both. There's nothing wrong with holding a strictly informational meeting—"three minutes each, over and out"—so long as opportunities are also provided for the play of ideas, whether incorporated into an informational meeting such as a weekly staff meeting, or held separately.

Meetings are a prime tool used by senior management to execute their goals.

So, what do CEOs know about meetings that we don't? Well, actually there are two secrets. The first involves "meetings-craft": how to make any meeting a genuinely productive event, and ensure a return on the time investment of the brainpower in attendance. The second secret is the "value-driven" meeting. Later in the chapter, I'll reveal how executives enrich and deepen the impact of their meetings by pulling the best out of participants.

The Six Fundamentals of Meetings-Craft

Let's start with something all managers and executives can agree upon: Executing a well-run meeting is a craft. Here is a story of a meeting that worked:

Weekly Meetings and Why You Need Them

Several years ago I visited the executive of a consulting organization employing about sixteen people. She walked me through her offices in a lovely old converted Victorian house near Long Island Sound. When we returned to her private office, I remarked, "You don't have weekly staff meetings, do you?"

"How did you know that?" she exclaimed.

Much as I'd like to claim magical powers, it was pretty apparent. Based on our short stroll through the office, I sensed too many things falling through the cracks on both the professional side and the office/admin areas, and the tension level was high.

For example, during our walkabout, the executive became visibly annoyed twice with staffers. In one case the person hadn't informed her about a glitch in the purchase of expensive equipment. The other occurred because she had been unaware until that moment that clients were complaining about excessive delays in callbacks.

Back in her office, I explained that these tensions and hangups were occurring because there was no forum or venue for the regular, systematic exchange of information and problem-solving. The organization's "on the fly" communication mode wasn't meeting their needs.

Like many managers, this executive had made the mistake of assuming that regular weekly meetings were a waste of time: How could we fit it in? Everyone's so busy . . .

Once the connection was drawn between the annoyance of frequently dropped balls and the lack of regular, face-to-face meetings, she instituted them the very next week. Because these meetings had to be inserted before the working day began, which meant a very early start for everyone, the executive softened the early-morning command performance by sending out a memo in advance stating the goals, purpose, and structure of the meeting. She also warmed the meeting by bringing coffee and doughnuts, and by encouraging participants to weigh in on the form and format of the meeting itself to make sure it was a productive use of their time.

DIFFERENT MEETING STYLES

Kent Crawford, CEO of PM Solutions in Havertown, PA, holds his weekly staff meeting by conference call on Fridays at 7:30 a.m. The meeting with his eleven directors and vice-presidents, who are scattered all over the country, usually lasts somewhat over an hour.

Crawford focuses the meeting to ensure that everyone is aware of what's going on, and to set up a "forum" so executives can have feedback from one another and assist each other in things they might need to do.

* * *

Juliana Rondina of the New York State Department of Education pointed out that because her primary job and that of her associates is to be out in the schools, they don't have weekly staff meetings. So she and her working group have an all-day meeting in one month, and then, in the alternate month, they hold a division-wide meeting.

* * *

Andrew Grove points out in the 1990 *Fortune* article that regularly scheduled meetings with subordinates are a timesaver because they'll save their routine questions and comments for the weekly session, and won't interrupt you as much.

When the staff saw how much more smoothly the wheels turned after the meetings got under way, all complaints ceased. For example, at that very first meeting, a method was devised to "triage" client calls by using color-coded message slips, ensuring that urgent calls were returned promptly, and that all calls were returned within twenty-four hours.

According to Grove, the only difference between pointless meetings and productive ones is the magic word *discipline*. By that he is referring to the disciplines of an effective meeting and how to execute them.

Most executives agree that productive meetings share six fundamental elements:

1. *A written agenda*, distributed in advance, so that participants know what materials to bring, and are prepared to discuss the topics at hand.

2. *Beginning and ending on time.*

3. *Strong leadership* to encourage participation, while keeping the meeting from veering off course.

4. *No loose ends.* Meetings can flounder quickly if matters are raised only to be left hanging. Every subject brought up needs to be carried to a next action—even if that action is simply to table or discard it.

5. *Meeting notes.* All decisions and assignments should be written up and distributed, ideally the same day.

6. *Follow-up.* It is essential to address the preceding meeting's "outstanding business" at the next meeting or in another appropriate venue.

From my interviews and research I've culled a wide range of specific tactics to accomplish these six fundamentals.

CREATING AN AGENDA

An agenda-less meeting is a prescription for major timewaste. Agendas can range from no-frills—for example, the notes from last week's weekly staff meeting—to (for a formal quarterly meeting) materials in a binder backed up by elaborate documentation.

Andrew Grove says, "Force the leaders of all meetings to determine what three or four points they want to make. Have them put in a certain amount of planning—I mean at least ten minutes. And if someone walks into the meeting with 600 [slides], you have to be strong enough to say, 'Hey, this is bullshit. Next time bring no more than ten or fifteen, and give us some time to discuss what you present.'"

Whether casual or complex, having an agenda in hand launches the meeting on the right foot by ensuring that participants know what materials to bring and are prepared to discuss the topics on the table. Here are two executives' different approaches to agenda creating:

Dennis Bass, deputy director of the Washington, D.C.–based Center for Science in the Public Interest, maintains a "running memo" on his computer. Items to discuss are entered contemporaneously, as he thinks of them, or as other people propose items for discussion.

Then Bass will pull the items that need to be discussed at *that* week's meeting. Some of the remaining items on his running agenda

TWO AGENDA TIPS

- Speed up agenda creation by taking advantage of calendar software programs such as Microsoft's Outlook, which provides considerable space for creating bulleted agenda items or notes in advance of your meeting.

- Assign an agenda item to each participant in the form of a problem and a proposed solution.

SPEEDY MEETING TIP

To keep latecomers from disrupting the conversational flow, place a copy of the agenda and handouts on each chair.

---

might be deleted as not adding value, while the others are tabled for a future meeting.

Dr. Julie Flagg, head of a multi-physician practice in Middletown, Connecticut, creates weekly staff meeting agendas by tilling the ground in advance, either in person or by phone. To prepare for the Monday staff meeting, she will informally discuss with colleagues a couple of key items on the preceding Thursday and Friday. Thus everyone is already aware of ideas that will be floated, and can prepare accordingly.

BEGINNING AND ENDING ON TIME

Here's how three executives make sure their meetings start on time:

- An Atlanta banking executive recommends this tactic in a *Business 2.0* article: "I say very politely, 'I was here at nine o'clock. I'm sorry you were late, but I'm going to have to leave on schedule at nine-thirty.' That sends a message and usually speeds up the meeting."

- Jack Gallaway says, "My people know that if I have a meeting and they're one minute late, I'll send my assistant after them."

- Another executive, to prevent people from arriving late, asks his assistant to call attendees fifteen minutes ahead of time to say, "The meeting is about to begin." He sits facing the door so that all latecomers will meet his gaze when entering the room (a strong deterrent for repeat latecomers).

Ending promptly is a fetish with some executives.

- Arthur Levitt, chairman of the SEC in the Clinton administration, says, "I run a very efficient meeting. It starts to the *second,* because that can raise a message. And anyone coming to a meeting with me knows *exactly* what time it's going to end—not one minute late, and sometimes early. If we can finish in a half hour, the meeting is *over.* I can't endure an open-ended meeting. I just hate them . . . Certainly meetings that I can control are very tightly controlled."

- Entrepreneur and turnaround expert Gary Sutton suggests when the agenda is distributed before the meeting, indicate how much time you will spend with each subject, and stick to it.

- General Motors president and CEO Rick Wagoner recommends: "At meetings, we have one hour to decide what we're going to do, and who's going to do it. Presentations and questions have to be submitted beforehand so we can focus on the important ones."

- Jim Morris of Signator keeps his meetings crisp because he has about fourteen of them a day. So he has made it clear he likes the *"Reader's Digest* version."

STRONG LEADERSHIP

A rudderless meeting is the very definition of a timewaster. But effectively leading a meeting is a little like negotiating a minefield. Encouraging the free expression of views, while keeping the meeting on track, is a balancing act.

There are different views on this point of encouraging free expression. Arthur Levitt and Rick Wagoner, in their remarks above, make a strong point about tightly controlling meeting length, which requires that participants make their points quickly, then over and out.

In support of that view, Steve Kaye, in *The Manager's Pocket Guide to Effective Meetings,* suggests limiting each attendee to two-minute updates. Use a timer to enforce your rule, if you need to. Allow three minutes of questions after each speaker. That leads the group to pose concise, specific queries.

Rick Cronk, president of Dreyer's Grand Ice Cream, to encourage people to keep their remarks on point, tapes twenty-dollar bills to the conference room wall. Any manager who completes his or her presentation early can take a bill off the wall on the way out.

But there's a contrarian side to the "short and sweet" meeting strategy. One executive I spoke to roundly criticized his manager, who routinely cut people off at staff meetings and did not explore the full range of views of people attending. He observed: "Our job is to support her in supporting us by giving her the benefit of our experience and ideas. But she's cutting us off at the knees in the service of making meetings short. I think that's a big mistake. And it's beginning to show. She's made some poor decisions simply because her information was too limited, and we've suffered some unnecessary reverses because of those decisions."

What's the solution?

My observation is that over-restricting opportunities for the free play of ideas is a mistake that can come back to bite you. But the logistics of making time for this essential creative thinking varies depending on the manager's preference. You might consider integrating a brainstorming or "idea play" element into regular weekly staff meetings. On the other hand, keeping your weekly meetings tight so long as you open things up with, perhaps, monthly free-form meetings can be equally productive.

NO LOOSE ENDS

Meetings can founder quickly if topics are raised, only to be left dangling. Dennis Bass reports, "If someone raises a question or reservation about a course of action during a meeting, I'll never just let it lie there. I'll ask him or her to get together with a few staffers before

RESURFACING ISSUES UNTIL YOU GET THEM RIGHT

I was intrigued by Dr. Julie Flagg's insistence on developing a solution for every concern by "resurfacing" items over and over until they are either incorporated, modified, or dropped. At each meeting the team asks, "How's it going?" for each initiative. Some ideas are "bombs," while others are "keepers."

For example, to make things easier for the billing department, they first tried a system of using red pens so physicians could tick off certain items on their "superbills." But switching from red pens for billing to black pens for prescriptions became cumbersome—the idea bombed. So the team tried switching to a highlighting method, which proved to be a big winner.

My takeaway on this method of "resurfacing" was that two things were being accomplished: practical problems were being solved; and at the same time, by creating a forum for discussions and concerns of this kind, a *team* was being forged—bonds were being established to create a cooperative, collaborative endeavor.

the next meeting to completely resolve the problem and report on the results at the next meeting. I'll put it into the notes so the matter doesn't get lost."

MEETING NOTES AND FOLLOW-UP

Choose one person to take note of decisions made, tasks assigned, and due dates. When assigning tasks, Jack Gallaway has a clever strategy: when possible, he instructs, "Pick any date you want and add two weeks to it." By choosing the due date themselves, his staff members have accepted responsibility. They also know that once a date is set, his tracking system is infallible.

Choose one person to summarize and distribute notes. Gaston Caperton takes his own meeting notes on a Compaq Tablet, so they are instantly distributable to attendees.

Be sure everyone agrees to report on progress at the next meeting, using the minutes or notes from the previous meeting as your guide. That may sound like a no-brainer—not one executive I spoke with would dream of neglecting these closers—but you'd be surprised how many people do. Neglecting to close the loop is like putting a sign up saying, "We've just agreed to dribble away a half hour or more of our time uselessly—and we didn't even have fun."

One senior executive at the William Morris Agency stays abreast of things by having each department—which includes TV, theater, movies, and a literary agency—send him the minutes of each department's meetings each week.

No matter what your position or ambitions, you can still operate like a CEO in your own realm by following the six fundamentals of productive meetings. They're a proven guide for getting the most out of the time spent in any group session.

Solving Problems That Can Derail Meeting Productivity

We've all been in meetings that ended up seriously off-track due to one of these problems:

- Rambling
- Agenda-busting, which occurs when a legitimate but unexpected issue arises that, if explored at the meeting, throws the meeting off-track.
- Using the meeting as an inappropriate venue for conflict, grandstanding, politics, airing of grievances, etc.

Here are some ways in which top executives keep meetings on track:

RAMBLING

Exchange of views is one thing. Dithering is another. During my day shadowing John Curley at Gannett, at one meeting I attended with him, when one participant seemed to be rambling, he declared crisply, "Let's move on." Another executive's pet phrase is "Let's wrap it up in the next ten words."

Robert Hemenway, chancellor of the University of Kansas, will generally use humor to pull the meeting back on course. He might say something like "You know, that's a great solution to the problem of the Middle East, but it doesn't do much for the freshman class at the University of Kansas." Everybody has a laugh, and focus is restored.

AGENDA-BUSTING

Robert Hemenway's preference, when something unexpected comes up during a meeting, is to nominate a task force, saying something like "Joe, Jane, and Jerry, draw upon whatever help you need, and prepare a report for discussion at our next meeting."

HANDLING CONFLICT

One executive at a large construction firm told me, "In our industry, too many meetings are called to paper over differences that need to be hashed out between individuals. I insist the individuals meet first, and then findings can be presented at our next regular meeting."

Here's how one executive handled a situation that threatened to split his team: "Two of my guys hate each other's guts. One says 'black' and the other says 'white'—all the while hurling invective at each other. This antagonism was shutting down any real debate. So I worked up a process that made it possible for them to work together, and I delivered an ultimatum: Do this or you're both out of here.

"When they receive the agenda a couple of days before the meeting, they have to briefly review it beforehand together to sketch out their positions on the various items.

SIMPLE QUESTIONS TO MAKE
YOUR MEETINGS MORE EFFECTIVE

- "What's the meeting's purpose?" What seems obvious to you may not be for those who attend your meetings. If, for example, everyone feels that the meetings are just designed to deliver status reports on information everybody already knows, then they may consider it timewaste. So get to the bottom of your folks' thinking by going around the table asking everyone to address that question.
- "What, if anything, prevents us from reaching the meeting's goal?" Are key information holders missing? Does the meeting last too long or is it too short?
- "How can we overcome these obstacles?" This is the perfect opportunity for participants to suggest changes they've been thinking about.

Suggestion: If you think your staffers might prefer *not* to openly discuss all problems, ask them to anonymously fill out a questionnaire based on these three questions.

And here are two tips from Peter F. Drucker, adapted from his book *The Effective Executive:*

- At the beginning of each meeting, state its purpose and the outcome you want to achieve. At the end of the meeting, compare what actually happened with your opening statement. You will quickly see where and how you wandered off course.
- Reserve the last ten minutes of each meeting to ask, "What should we do next?" and to delegate tasks. If you focus only on past issues and current problems, you'll overlook the most important time frame: the future.

"Then they have to prepare a brief joint position paper simply listing in bullet points the three or four or five options they've jointly come up with—without identifying whose position is which. Then, in the meetings, I insist that they are polite to each other. So, bottom line, though they'll always dislike each other—I don't know why, they're both nice, competent guys—forcing them to work together has had three benefits: it has lowered the decibel level and team factionalism; it has preserved their ability to continue as productive members of our working community—an ability that was rapidly eroding; and unexpectedly, some fresh and interesting ideas have emerged from their joint communiqués."

In her book *More Team Gains for Trainers,* Carolyn Wilson suggests quelling conflict during meetings with the word "what." Examples: "What makes you ask?" "What bothers you about that?" People generally drop fixed positions or hostility when asked to clarify their positions.

More Inventive Meetings Tips from Executives

INVITE PEOPLE STRATEGICALLY

Make sure the people who need to be there are present, and structure the meeting so that participants can leave when their portion is concluded and they are no longer needed.

Have more short meetings with decision-makers only. Invite only the decision-makers on a problem, and meet with them for only fifteen minutes. This is a better use of time than a Cecil B. DeMille–style staff meeting where the "extras" sit around until it's their moment to throw a spear.

One senior vice-president of Investor Communications, Smith Barney Inc., suggests, "Two groups of people need to be considered in connection with meetings: the critical people, who'll make the decisions or contribute something substantial; and those who only need to know the outcome after the fact. I only invite the critical group, calling or e-mailing them in advance, to tell them (1) the purpose—what we hope to accomplish; (2) what specifically is expected of each person in the meeting—why they're invited, what I expect them to do, and any materials they should bring.

"Then, after the meeting, I distribute FYI memos to the second group, the need-to-knows, summarizing any decisions made or conclusions arrived at, and also any steps that need to be taken."

BLOCK OUT MEETING TIME

Dennis Bass of the D.C.-based Center for Science in the Public Interest blocks out periods of meeting time so as to open up periods for creative work such as reviewing marketing materials.

To fit it all in, Bass works to focus *all* his regular monthly meetings with his direct reports within two days.

MEETING SETTINGS

Many executives feel that physical aspects of the meeting place are an important productivity factor. One manager I know deliberately holds her staff meetings in a cramped space, because the forced proximity makes her people more vigorous and lively. Here are some additional ideas:

Hold meetings at the source. Melia Peavey, COO of Peavey Electronics Corp., a manufacturer of electronic musical instruments in Meridien, Mississippi, calls many meetings at the location of the topic under discussion. If it's a production problem, attendees assemble on the production floor; if it's a warehouse matter, the discussion is held there. "When you're cooped up in a meeting room, the problem seems remote," Peavey observed. "By going to the site, you get decisions rolling quickly . . . and employees are impressed that management is involved and not sitting in offices looking down on everything."

You can shake things up by holding working sessions in unexpected settings.

Meet over a meal. In his autobiography, *Iacocca,* Lee Iacocca tells how the idea for the Ford Mustang—the car that jumpstarted his career—emerged from intense conversations about "the next big car" during regular weekly dinners "with the guys" at a local restaurant.

Meet at a "dump." Jerry McLaughlin, CEO of Branders.com, a Foster City, California, firm that sells promotional productions, holds staff meetings at Redneck Earl's—a "dump" where beer comes in mason jars and you eat with your hands.

McLaughlin says many key decisions—from hiring to picking the location for a new headquarters—were made at Earl's.

Create a fantasy setting. Peter Kirwan, chief technology officer at NaviSite, a web-hosting company in Andover, Massachusetts, installed a fake fireplace in his office, put candles on the mantel, and invited employees over for hot chocolate. "All of a sudden, people were coming up with great [problem-solving] ideas," he states.

Making Meetings Productive When You're Not in Charge

So now you've got a pretty good idea about how senior executives conduct their meetings. But how can you adapt what you have learned from them to heighten your ability to be an effective participant in, and extract value from, meetings that other people run? Invigorate your ability to make meeting time productive time in two ways: proactively and defensively.

Being proactive. "Doing meetings well," bottom line, is a matter of figuring out what is expected of you by your manager and acting accordingly. Here are three things to look at:

- *Participation style.* Though virtually all managers promote the virtues of active participation, scope out whether your manager prefers people to jump right in, or whether he or she prefers to call on people and generally run a more regulated meeting.

- *Tolerance for dissension.* Figure out your boss's comfort level with open slugging it out when people disagree. Some people love it and are invigorated by raised-voice dissension. Others can't stand it.
- *Tone and personal style.* Be aware of personal quirks such as tending to go on too long, or interrupting or overriding others.

One executive told me that he had planned to bring along with him, as he began his rise, someone who worked for him. But this person continually interrupted others at meetings—and didn't correct himself even when the fault was pointed out to him several times. So the executive reluctantly left the man behind, feeling that his tendency to override others, combined with his inability to take direction, did not equip him for a higher position.

By raising your consciousness, you are not only helping your team and boss have a successful meeting, but you are gaining skill and confidence in your own ability to run a productive meeting.

Applying the "six fundamentals" when you're not in charge. Here are my tips on how to exercise influence over the six fundamentals. You have more maneuvering room than you may think:

1. *Be sure you have a written agenda.* If you haven't received an agenda for an important meeting by two days in advance, don't get blindsided. Ask the person in charge. If the response is fuzzy, try this tactic:

If political ramifications permit, consider saying to the meeting's leader, "I've got a couple of things on my plate—would it work to put them on the agenda?"

That way, without the leader's realizing it, you have shifted the agenda—or perhaps created an agenda where there wasn't one.

2. *Begin and end on time.* If you feel a meeting is dragging, but the person in charge isn't taking the reins, help bring it to closure in a collaborative way by saying something like "Gee, guys, remember there was something we wanted to talk about later? I'd better collect my materials pretty soon. They're kind of spread out and I have to organize them. What's our next important topic here at this meeting?" Taking the initiative gives you a pretty good shot at breaking the meeting up.

3. *Take strong leadership.* If a meeting has become boring or rudderless, do your best, within the range of your position and authority, still to make the time productive. Try these three tactics:

- Spark a lively discussion. Ask something like "Jerry, I was thinking that taking this tack rather than that one might have some advantages. Could you give us your views about the likely outcome of the two alternatives?"

- As you sit there, consider your colleagues. What is your best guess as to their hopes and aspirations? What are their strongest individual skills and their weakest? With which colleagues can you forge productive partnerships? Are there rivalries or oppositional relationships? Dallas's Ted Benavides said, "When you're in a meeting and you're not the leader, I always wanted to learn everything about what my colleagues were doing so that if they weren't there and my boss asked me if I could help . . . And I got better by knowing stuff that wasn't within my area of expertise. And so, now that I'm the boss, I know so much about this place—it just helps me in every way."

- Do other work. Actually, I only recommend this at a mind-numbing large meeting where no one is apt to be paying attention to you.

**SUMMARY OF THE SIX FUNDAMENTALS
OF AN EFFECTIVE MEETING**

1. Be sure you have a written agenda.
2. Begin and end on time.
3. Take strong leadership.
4. Leave nothing hanging.
5. Take meeting "notes" or minutes.
6. Follow up on all outstanding matters.

4. *Leave nothing hanging.* If the meeting leader isn't making sure items are being resolved one way or another, interject a comment such as "What's the next step on that project? Could you please clarify?"

5. *Take notes.* Operate on defense: take your own notes!

6. *Follow up.* Again, keep track of who is to do what on your own if the leader is not doing so. If you need someone to carry out a piece of the action before you can take your own next step, talk to him or her before the next meeting.

Trading Up: Along the Arc of Executive Possibility

Value-added meetings

Every manager from new-hire to CEO defines the armature of an effective meeting by the six strategies of meetings-craft we have just discussed.

Yet, in addition to meetings-craft, I discovered that, as you rise to within striking distance of the executive suite, something begins to look different. In a word—or two words—think "think tank": meetings intended to tap great ideas and galvanize commitment.

In his book (with Ram Charan) *Execution: The Discipline of Getting Things Done,* Larry Bossidy, who cut his teeth as one of Jack Welch's inner circle at GE and went on to become chairman and CEO of Honeywell International, says, "Think about the meetings you've attended— those that were a hopeless waste of time and those that produced energy and great results. What was the difference? . . . The difference was in the quality of the dialogue"—what Bossidy calls the "live ammo."

Top executives look to pull out a depth of information, a fecundity of ideas, and a vital, even exciting, interchange between the participants that brings a certain depth of commitment, interest, and excitement that you couldn't otherwise achieve.

I first saw this in action when I attended a meeting led by Joseph Vittoria at Avis with five or six of his marketing people. They were meeting to discuss the upcoming year's allocation of advertising dollars.

Mr. Vittoria went into action posing deliberative questions like these: "Pulling out this tactic you proposed, how do you think it might impact Kinney and Hertz?"; "What if we reversed position and went about it this way, instead of that way?"; "Let me play devil's advocate. What downside do you see to this approach?"

The thinking and engagement he generated were exciting! By engaging his people at a galvanized level, Mr. Vittoria created a lively forum that added value to an otherwise pretty routine meeting.

Four Ways to Leverage Meeting Value

Based on my observations, executives utilize four strategies to achieve the state of "think tank." None are mutually exclusive:

1. Drawing out great ideas through strategic questions.
2. Practicing "creative dissonance."

THREE WAYS TO FRAME SEARCHING QUESTIONS

1. "And the reason [product defects have increased sharply] is . . . ?"
2. "Are we doing anything that makes it difficult for us to [meet our numbers?] [challenge our competitor's new product?]"
3. What can we do to [make it better?] [strengthen our position?]"

3. Pulling out the raw facts and unfiltered opinion.
4. Thinking rich—taking a different approach to time.

Drawing Out Great Ideas Through Strategic Questions

Frank Wells, president of Disney under Michael Eisner until his death in 1994, was a master at extracting good and fresh ideas from his direct reports through provocative questions. For example, he said to a colleague, "Excuse me. Excuse me. Can you conceive of a situation where you won't be panicked with this budget?"

Later, meeting with construction managers who reported that everything was going fabulously, he said, "Okay, okay. Give me one negative thing. Where does it say in here whether or not we're on budget?"

What he pulled from his folks seemed to be in the nature of scenarios, which helped people reframe their situation.

John Curley of Gannett took a similar tack at one of his meetings I attended.

He kept asking questions like "Which did you think worked best?", "What pitfalls do you see?", "What are the challenges?"—not to challenge or confront, but simply to pull out a greater depth or complexity of thought.

Practicing "Creative Dissonance"

Some successful executives actively solicit the clash of ideas and "creative dissonance" as a vehicle for bringing out the full range of ideas and possibilities.

Chief William J. Bratton of the LAPD says, "People understand that I want open discussion—I invite and encourage it. Differences of opinion are not something I frown on . . ." One reason he fosters such dissonance is to reduce the ability to withhold or filter information.

In the bestseller *Good to Great,* author Jim Collins lauds Nucor Steel CEO Ken Iverson for encouraging intense debate. General manager meetings "were chaos," Iverson said. "We'd stay there for hours, ironing out the issues . . . People yelled. They waved their arms around and pounded on tables." But they always emerged with a conclusion. An Enron-type situation, where people were lying and withholding up and down the line, could never have occurred in this atmosphere of open debate.

Pulling Out the Raw Facts and Unfiltered Opinions

The drive to retrieve raw facts and unfiltered opinions is also behind another executive meeting strategy: speak last, not first.

Luke Corbett, CEO of the Kerr-McGee Oil Company in Oklahoma City, never mentions what he thinks about a matter until everyone has aired his or her view. His reasoning is that because he's the boss, once he says something, people will unconsciously distort their thinking to conform to his—and he wants their unbiased thoughts.

CONSENSUAL VERSUS NON-CONSENSUAL DECISION STYLES

Meetings of a manager and direct reports are not a democracy. Chancellor Hemenway mostly operates in the consensual mode, but reserves the right to override. "If you're absolutely certain it's right and you're the one who has been delegated the authority . . . you go ahead and make that decision, even though out of ten people there may be only two that agree with you. But if you do that very often—if more than five to ten percent of your decisions are made that way— you've probably got a dysfunctional organization, because you're not depending enough on the wisdom that's available from your support group."

Thinking Rich: Taking a Different Approach to Time

In defining what constitutes an effective, productive meeting, many top executives concentrate on the quality of what emerges, rather than on the time spent. I call this quality outcome "rich-think." But executive rich-think can take more time than the short, crisp meetings most of us regard as productive.

To be honest, I was surprised by how many executives favor long meetings—*really* long meetings—on a regular basis.

At Duke Energy, top executives find great value in extremely long meetings. CEO Chris Rolfe says much of his work gets done in the biweekly, day-long policy committee meetings. "It's much more ongoing and real-time . . . we're updating these plans every day because our organization is so dynamic."

Said Robert Crandall, former CEO of American Airlines, "I want the chance to ask [a person] a thousand questions. That simply cannot be done without bringing people together."

What's the Takeaway?

Whether or not you are aiming for the boardroom, we summarize here three signature concepts that are shared by people who possess this mindset about value-driven, think-tank meetings.

1. Understand the meeting culture in your own company. Keep alert for what works and what doesn't.

2. Contribute as best you can to the content, flow, and follow-up of each meeting. Be mindful of your own ability to affect events.

3. Determine what your own personal "meeting style" is, so that you can implement it effectively when you are the one in charge.

Now, even if it isn't your style, you can fathom where your boss is coming from in meetings, and have a better idea of what is expected from you during these sessions. Remember, too, that with so many managers today being B-schooled, the think-tank notion is often deeply ingrained into their mentality.

And if you are keeping an eye on the executive suite, some familiarity with these four strategies CEOs use to elicit big ideas can help you make meetings maximally productive.

13

The Curious Power
of Interruptions

. . .

Surprisingly, CEOs insist that welcoming drop-ins to their office, not shutting them out, can be one of their most potent managerial tools. I discovered this apparently contrarian notion by accident.

Over the past few years I have been "shadowing" a select number of this country's leading CEOs during typical days in their offices to gain insight into their organizational and time-management strategies.

One of the first executives I studied was Joseph V. Vittoria, who at the time served as chairman & CEO of Avis. Mr. Vittoria's day began as I surmised a busy CEO's would: going over his calendar of appointments with his secretary, processing paperwork, returning phone calls, etc.

But soon I noticed something odd—his day seemed to have become entirely unstructured. Outside of about two and a half hours of calendared meetings and appointments, his time seemed to consist of an endless series of interruptions—direct reports casually dropping by to discuss matters that had arisen, phone calls from colleagues inside and outside the company, and forays out and about on the floor—classic MBWA.

This constant round of unplanned events didn't throw him in the least. When I asked him how, as the executive in charge of a huge corporation with so many responsibilities, he was able to handle all these interruptions to his workday without getting irritated, he shot me a quizzical look. At the time I ascribed his strange response to an idiosyncratic attitude. I proceeded on with my study by "tailing" John Curley, then CEO of Gannett, for a day. I soon noticed that, as with Mr. Vittoria, his day consisted of only about two and a half hours of scheduled appointments, with the balance left open for these same kinds of nonstop "interruptions."

Interesting. Here were two highly successful executives from disparate industries—rental cars and newspapers—who both ran their days by a deliberate if unconscious combination of structure and looseness.

As my "Day in the Life of a CEO" study continued, I began probing other executives on this topic, and discovered that almost all of them operated in the same fashion. It simply didn't make sense to me. I had assumed that senior executives' days would be tightly calendared, and that their direct reports would have severely limited access.

Instead, I found exactly the opposite to be true: at the very top, there was a complete freedom on the part of the executive's direct reports and immediate associates—a circle of maybe fifteen people—to come and go.

When I asked executives the reasons for this seemingly contradictory mindset, the pattern seemed so natural that none of them were able to cite a specific rationale.

Then I was fortunate to interview Dr. George E. Pickett, then State Health Commissioner of West Virginia and past president of the American Public Health Association. Perhaps because of his academic background, he was able to articulate an answer. When I asked him how he handled interruptions, he retorted, "What interruptions?"

I described the scenarios I had observed, and he went on to explain, "What you are calling 'interruptions' *is* my work. From the beginning of my career, I have seen my job as being available to facilitate, troubleshoot, run ideas by, solve problems, and just be a presence. If I had an urgent deadline, I would go into a conference room and shut the door. But that rarely happens."

At that moment I had a Fortune 500 epiphany: *The very incessant interruptions that drive most managers insane were to him and other CEOs the very lifeblood of their day.* Organizational leaders, it seems, don't view interruptions the same way the rest of us do.

Take, for example, these comments from Ted Benavides in Dallas. Benavides doesn't even try for private time during the day. Here is what he said: "If no one's in my office, I'll start looking for people . . . My job is to communicate with my staff, my bosses, and my customers—the citizens. It's my job to walk around, touching [base with] the rank and file.

"Okay, I'm making myself available, but I need to be more mobile. I need to be out in the field more . . . I *want* to see the animal shelter. Yesterday I went out to see one of our air-monitoring stations . . ."

My initial reaction to this fascinating finding was that senior executives' ability to juggle the unexpected and unplanned was a luxurious perk of sitting at the top with legions of staff at their disposal.

But the truth that ultimately emerged proved surprising: people who climb the rungs of large organizations to the top have practiced an active "open door" policy from their very first job. *By making themselves available to all the people around them, they become an epicenter of influence, a human centrifugal force that can, with talent, hard work, and a bit of luck, propel them up the line.*

At first blush, the notion of inviting "interruptions" appears antithetical to the concept of efficient time management. But the more I observed these leaders at close range, the more I realized that by structuring their time in a way that invites others to seek their opinion, advice, or help, they inadvertently create the means by which they attain success—and, in many cases, higher office. From the start, their willingness to interact at a moment's notice sends the message that they are in control, which over time becomes a self-fulfilling prophecy.

All of this may be fascinating, but from your standpoint it might not sound terribly practical. At this point in your career path, chances are you can't afford to have people popping in and out, hijacking your day. Facing these two seemingly contradictory goals—being accessible to colleagues and proactively shaping your own day—is a tricky balancing act.

The secret lies in understanding that there are really only three basic "interruption styles." Determining which one best suits your persona is key to maximizing your productivity up and down the management line at work.

The Three "Interruption Styles"

Channeling interactions and interruptions is an often annoying but necessary aspect of any job today. I have identified three basic "interruption styles" practiced by corporate managers to help them achieve maximum productivity. Before each one, I describe the "hallmark" attitude that best exemplifies that mindset, to help you identify your own "interruption style."

1. All Interruptions, All the Time

> **Hallmark:** *You maintain an open-door policy on a regular basis, welcoming and even inviting spontaneous interaction with colleagues, staff, customers, and those up and down the line.*
>
> *Unexpected demands on your time to discuss problems, opportunities, or ongoing business are what make you tick. You take care of*

your other essential work before or after office hours, which often necessitates fourteen- to fifteen-hour days.

Many executives *need* interruptions to keep them apprised hour-by-hour of the important things that are going on in their own company and in their industry.

Joseph Vittoria told me that when someone wasn't waiting to see him, he walked out and asked his assistant, "Who's next?" To a CEO, incessant contact *is* the real work. The torrent of questions, comments, updates, requests, and expectations—perhaps hundreds a day—is a rich resource to be mined. The constant engagement can be a process through which you enable colleagues—which comes back to you as a benefit in myriad ways, large and small.

Donald Guinn of Pacific Telesis, for example, described the many demands on his time as a "menu of opportunity" from which he can select in performing his job.

Akira Chiba of Pokémon USA emphasizes MBWA, briefly touching base with the folks in his office building at every opportunity.

Numerous other executives told the same story. Andrew Grove refers to leaving substantial "air pockets" of time each day open to what may come his way. Joseph Dionne, when he headed McGraw-Hill, scheduled no calendared meetings at all with his direct reports, simply leaving his door open for them on an as-needed basis—which made for dozens of drop-bys.

Remember, though, there is a method to this madness. *Spontaneous interaction is the work of the CEO. Many of America's top executives govern their companies—gather information, problem-solve, exert influence, and facilitate priority goals—through the casual, unscripted contacts the rest of us call interruptions.*

This "all interruptions, all the time" mindset isn't limited to CEOs; people at all levels and situations operate this way spontaneously. For example, Todd Cowgill of Pekin Insurance is equally responsive.

"Employees usually call on me because they need help," he says. So, for most of the workday, he considers it appropriate to make himself available to employees who need him.

A senior editor at a publishing company once described a frustrating moment of disconnect with her boss. She peeked into his office one day to ask him a question, and thoughtfully stood in his doorway for a few moments while he tapped away intently at his computer, so as not to interrupt him. Once he saw her, he became annoyed, asking impatiently, "Why didn't you just come in?" When she explained, he replied, "But that's my job—to be available! Whether it's a question, a roadblock we need to hash out, or just to bounce some ideas around, that's what I'm here for."

This severe disconnect, which baffled and distressed her, illustrates how important it is to understand the mindset of your supervisor, and the expectations he or she has about how to carry on basic communications during the course of the day. And there's a lesson here, too, about being available to your colleagues. Starting to view interruptions as an opportunity to enable or help someone else in his or her own work is a great way to increase your own value in your company.

So, how do executives signal to staff and colleagues that their doors are open?

- *Their door is literally wide open.* An open door signals that you welcome people to stop in with questions, problems, or advice.
- *They maintain a comfortable seating area.* Never stack anything on or around your chairs that would make it hard for people to sit down. President Reagan kept a big jar of jelly beans on his desk.
- *They update their voice-mail message every day.* By providing callers with a brief update on your schedule, you let them know when they can count on you and where they can find you if they need you.

CEO CONTRARIAN: WILL HIS TOTAL CONTROL WORK?

Many readers of *Organized for Success* have the desire to escalate their ability to control their daily time schedule, in the belief that that will allow them to be most productive.

You are in good company. Steve Ballmer, Microsoft CEO since Bill Gates turned over the reins in 2001, loves his spreadsheet-based scheduling system. In a 2002 *New York Times Magazine* article, Ballmer says, "I'm religious about the way I manage my time." He adds that "the assemblage of tiny grids is . . . a necessary practicality of the way he must . . . go about his job. With the far-flung Microsoft products and markets, there is simply no way he can be the old-fashioned, be-everywhere boss he would otherwise like to be." Ballmer works out time allocations a year at a time on his scheduling sheet. Some examples for one year:

Selling: 48 days in the field

E-mail: 180 days @ 60 minutes per day plus plane trips

Staff time: His VP for marketing gets twelve hours one-on-one
   for the year

Certainly, Ballmer has been very successful. But in my experience, this sort of very rigid control over time goes directly against the grain of intense CEO interplay with direct reports and colleagues.

Only time will tell how Ballmer's heavily booked calendar plays out, but I think he may conclude that this is not the optimal time pattern to accomplish his goals as a chief executive. If you want to control your time tightly, you may have to rethink whether that approach is going to allow you the flexibility necessary to accomplish your own goals.

One executive, Donald Nickelson of PaineWebber, positioned his secretary's desk so far away from his office that people looking in could bypass her completely.

Most CEOs I studied rise very early to accomplish their private work, so as to be completely available during the workday. It simply goes with the territory. The needs of your family and household may not permit you to do this, but it's almost always possible to set the alarm clock a half hour earlier and carve out some valuable personal work time.

2. The Balanced "Open House" Approach

Hallmark: *With this hybrid style, you don't resent people dropping in, but you want to create an efficient time-management operation in terms of your own workday and your colleagues'. You get a significant portion of your own work done during the workday, but still seek interaction time on a regular basis.*

Although you welcome spontaneous interaction, you will make an effort to keep your office off limits to interruptions for part of the day to give you time to access your priority tasks, unless the interruptions are urgent.

If this style sounds like you, your primary "interruptions tactic" is to negotiate your time-balance between open-door time and more-restricted time. Here are suggestions for balancing those requirements:

BALANCING ASSERTIVENESS WITH AVAILABILITY

- Set up daily "open house" hours—say from 3:00 to 5:00 p.m.—when the welcome mat is out for colleagues and staff to pop in and share what's on their minds.
- Kent Crawford, president and CEO of PM Solutions, finds the traditional "gotta minute?" drop-in visits disruptive for routine

matters. So, to balance the time he needs for his own work with high accessibility to staff and colleagues, "I'll ask my direct reports to e-mail me saying, 'Can I see you at 3:00?' or whatever. I'll then e-mail back as soon as I can, 'OK' or '3:00 doesn't work, but I'm available between 12:00 and 2:00.' This way I'm highly accessible and yet get to control my time. Of course, if there is something extremely pressing, they let me know right away."

- One "open house" executive will ask what the priority is— "Right away?" or "Can wait." If the latter, he'll e-mail them when to come.

- A related "negotiated" approach: "I really want to see you, but I'm working on something critical. Can you come back and noodle at one-thirty?" "No—it's critical." "Okay, five minutes now."

- Negotiate with your boss: "I'm working on this for you. Do you want me to break and talk about it now, or should we wait until later?"

- Jeanette Wagner of Estée Lauder describes her time-allocation techniques: "I control all my appointments myself. My secretary will give me at night a list of requests for my time, the date, and the topic. I may say 'Yes, no, no, no, no.' 'This person should see this person.' 'I don't need to see this person,' or, 'Fifteen minutes is enough here.' I don't let my day get given away by my assistant."

- Put an amusing sign on your door or desk: "Genius at work, 9:00–10:00. Please leave me a note, or drop by later."

3. Controlled Access

Hallmark: *When someone peeks in, you feel as if your day has abruptly been hijacked, and try to figure out how to get rid of the person as fast as you can so that you can get back to work. You're not antisocial, you're just one of those people who likes to focus intently on the matter at hand.*

THE DESK DISAPPEARING ACT:
NOW YOU SEE HIM, NOW YOU DON'T

The late William McGowan, founder of MCI, devised a strategic office furniture arrangement to register whether he was "in" or "out." He placed two desks in his office. One was visible from the door, the other wasn't. When he was seated at the visible desk, that was an invitation to drop in. When he couldn't be seen, that was a signal that he didn't want to be disturbed.

Suffice it to say most of you don't have two desks (yet!), but you can arrange your office in such a way as to provide yourself a corner out of view—say, with a small table or credenza where you can set a laptop or phone—giving the impression that you're not available at the moment, yet not closing yourself off from the world.

Although you'd prefer to keep total control, in a less-than-perfect office world, you accept that you'll have to endure interruptions now and then. So you request that people call or e-mail you, or give you advance notice of their need to see you.

One executive has two methods by which he keeps people from overwhelming him: he keeps the temperature in his office at sixty-two degrees so that people go in and out quickly; and he keeps no chairs in the office except his own, so that people quickly get uncomfortable and leave.

Other Ideas

- Turn your desk so that you don't have automatic eye contact with every passerby, which encourages chat.
- When colleagues come into your office for a chat, stand up as if you were leaving. Let them take the hint.

- To cut off chat, ask, "Is there anything further you need to know?"
- At a pause point, say, "Thanks for the information. I appreciate it." Then "tango" your visitor to the door.

INTERRUPTIONS ARE A TWO-WAY STREET

It's critical to know which "interruption style" best fits your own temperament. It's equally critical to understand the styles of your colleagues, staff, and superiors.

One magazine editor spent the first three months on the job suffering severe communication problems with her publisher because of a lack of response to her repeated e-mails seeking answers to pressing questions.

Frustrated, the editor finally asked the publisher, "Would you prefer to deal with me via phone when I have a problem in need of resolution?" The publisher quickly responded, "Yes!" It was as if the publisher herself hadn't realized that she didn't like to be interrupted via e-mail, but phone calls were absolutely fine.

Play to each staff member's preferences as a way to foster and enhance the best efforts of that individual. If your deputy is irritated by constant interruptions, and you stick your head in twenty times a day, you will not get his or her best work, since the person is forced to operate out of annoyance.

If, on the other hand, a direct report is much more receptive to interruptions, they might be insulted—and possibly become paranoid—if you don't stop by often. Input is the currency of their day, and they'd fear that they'd done something wrong and possibly that their job was in jeopardy.

The Art of Managing Interruptions

CEOs may love all interruptions, all the time, but let's get real: not all interruptions are created equal. People *do* pop in and "kidnap" your time when they should be handling a matter themselves. People do ramble, and need to be encouraged to cut to the chase. The challenge is to ensure that these encounters are brisk and productive—that you don't get hung up in long disquisitions, or in discussions of your colleague's kitchen renovation. So here is a roundup of productivity tips that will help you make the most of each contact and better manage interruptions and spontaneous contacts so that they work for you, and not against you.

WAS YOUR TIME WELL SPENT?

Someone pops in to go over something quickly. Thirty minutes later they're just leaving. Whom are you mad at? Was your time well spent? If so, why? If not, why not? If a person is absorbing your time nonproductively, figure out how to handle it better the next time.

Six "Three-Minute Interruption" Strategies
SETTING UP THE "QUICKIE"

- Set up a time contract: "I have ten minutes at four o'clock."
- When a staffer asks, "Do you have a minute?" Reply, "No, but I do have thirty seconds." This automatically cuts their request for your time in half, and limits their options: they can be brief and concise for thirty seconds, wait until later when you have more time, or ask someone else.
- Say to a colleague who's going on too long, "Please give me the short version," or "I've got another ten minutes, so let's make sure we deal with the critical issues."

- Avoid asking open-ended questions like "What's up?" Ask "What can I do for you?" instead.

CUTTING THEM OFF AT THE PASS

- Ask your assistant to interrupt and remind you of your next appointment at a prearranged point, to give you a way to exit gracefully. If you don't have an assistant, set alarms on your watch or computer to go off to give you a graceful out. Or you can simply say, "I'm sorry, but I have another appointment now."
- Frame the discourse by asking, "What do you want me to do?" or "What are *you* going to do?"

Reducing the Interruption Flow

- *Prepare standard responses to repetitive questions.* Andrew Grove points out, "If you can pin down what kind of interruptions you're getting, you can prepare standard responses for those that pop up most often." To cut down on repetitive questions, one manager posted on the department's computer bulletin board a chart called "The Ten Most Common Situations and How to Deal with Them."

- *Delegate authority.* Clarify for your direct reports the range of actions and decisions they are empowered to make without consulting you. You'll eliminate many interruptions and speed the flow of work through your unit.

- *Communicate in writing—yes, writing.* At Vollmer Public Relations in Houston, managers and their staffers created an efficient system to cut down on nonessential interruptions. In lieu of phoning or e-mailing each other throughout the day, they use special mauve pads to write non-urgent notes to each other. Everyone must abide by one important rule: Respond to all notes by the end of the day.

Keep Impromptu Meetings from Chewing Up Your Day

- *The fast exit strategy.* When John Reed was chairman of Citicorp, staffers noticed he usually dropped into their offices rather than summon them to his office. The reason: by arriving in their offices, he could exit on his own timetable. So the next time someone calls to say they're going to drop by, instead immediately offer, "I'll be right over." That way you can leave whenever you want.

- *Try to hold impromptu meetings in someone else's office.* It's easier to excuse yourself than to kick people out of your office.

- *Lean against the doorjamb of the office you're visiting.* Ready to move on? When someone you "need to talk to" passes by, take the opportunity to make an exit.

- *Make preemptive visits.* IBM manager Sharon Hill found that her frequent business trips led to heavy interruptions when she returned to the office. Staff members dropped in throughout the day to deliver updates, news, etc. Now, when she returns from a trip, she spends the first hour or two swinging by each of her team members' offices, giving them the chance to tell her anything important and give quick updates. When she is finished making the rounds, she posts a "Do Not Disturb" sign and catches up on her work, uninterrupted.

- *Generally speaking, make time every day for MBWA.* Simply stopping by people's desks to ask "What's up?" can keep small problems from escalating into big ones and, not so incidentally, head off many interruptions before they land in your office.

Creative Idea

Establish a "no interruptions" zone. Intel's headquarters' cafeteria serves as a meeting place and informal conference room for employees throughout the company. However, Intel's cafeteria has a special

TAKE A MINI-BREAK

Spend some quiet time occasionally to refresh and recharge yourself during a busy day—fifteen minutes if possible, but if you can't find that, take ten or even five.

Tell everyone, "I need ten minutes alone. Please don't interrupt unless it's an emergency." Then go into your office, and don't emerge until you've had your mini-break.

difference: small signs scattered around the room that say "One-on-One."

As Intel's Carlene Ellis explains in Sally Helgesen's book *The Web of Inclusion,* if you put a sign on your table, others "won't stop to chat, so you can be very private even though you're visible. You don't have to schedule a conference room, you just tell someone to meet you downstairs."

PART IV

USING CEO STRATEGIES IN YOUR OWN DOMAIN

• • •

14

Using CEO Strategies
in Your Own Domain

• • •

In reading about the organization and time-management strategies of executives who have risen to the top, you may have noticed some common threads running through the story. After studying a number of organizational leaders at close range, I discovered that they operate in a highly distinctive mental realm when it comes to organization and time management.

In my opinion, what CEOs are really doing in this different realm—the real focus of their time, their core and ongoing project—is what I call *managing influence*. I first started to understand this phenomenon during an interview with a CEO in which I repeatedly pressed him to describe his "tasks." Finally he got a bit testy and replied, "Look, there's just one traditional task I do: I edit drafts of speeches prepared by my speechwriter—and I do that mostly when I'm on a plane. Otherwise, no tasks."

His retort brought me up short. I finally got it. No tasks.

But in the next breath, I asked myself, "These guys aren't sitting around watching the flowers grow. So if they're not doing tasks, then what exactly *are* they doing?"

Because virtually all their time is spent with others, I deduced that their work had to be conducted in some way through these contacts. By shadowing them, I had discovered, as described earlier, that these contacts were very free-form, consisting mostly of suggestions, questions, observations, and eliciting their direct reports' views, interwoven with occasional chat about golf, family activities, etc.

What the CEOs were doing, I concluded, was not primarily ordering others, but *influencing* them through constant contact. So that became my focus: how CEOs use their time to guide their company by influencing others.

Managing Influence*

Since "managing influence" sounds pretty theoretical, you may wonder how this concept can possibly apply to you. But I assure you, incorporating it into your workday, to a greater or lesser extent as you choose, can shift your whole perspective about time. For starters, I want to stress that managing influence is, so far as I am aware, a behavior typical of all up-the-ladder CEOs—those who have made their way, rung by rung, to the top of a large organization—across business and industry lines.

How can you, if you wish to, adapt this notion of managing influence to boost your own productivity?

It requires a shift of emphasis. Whereas for most of us accomplishing tasks consistent with defined priorities is the dominant emphasis, CEOs and those on the way up shift their emphasis to influencing others. "Influencing" in this context simply means the ability to slightly affect someone else's attitude or behavior—to encourage,

---

*In developing the concept of "managing influence," I have consulted the work of John Kotter in his 1982 classic, *The General Managers,* and Andrew S. Grove in his 1983 book, *High Output Management.*

**HOW ONE MANAGER
MANAGED INFLUENCE IN TWO MINUTES**

It's amazing how much influence can come into play in a short period of time. John Kotter, in *The General Managers,* tells an amusing story of a high-rolling 120 seconds:

> "Jack Martin," on his way to a meeting, bumped into a staff member (who did not report to him) near the elevator. Using this opportunity, in a two-minute conversation he (a) asked two questions and received the information needed in return; (b) helped to reinforce their good relationship by sincerely complimenting the manager on something he had recently done; and (c) got the manager to agree to do something that Jack needed done.
>
> The agenda in Jack's mind guided him through this encounter. It allowed him to ask important questions and to make an important request for action.
>
> At the same time, his relationship with this member of his network allowed him to get the cooperation he needed to do all this so quickly.

nudge, reprimand, gain a buy-in—by personal communication, either face to face or by phone. (E-mail doesn't count.)

So, how are CEOs able to strike so many chords in such a brief period of time?

Because they have a clear agenda in their minds, usually based primarily on executing the company's strategic plan, CEOs have the ability to achieve an unusually complex mining of "value" from virtually every interchange, including the most casual elevator chat, to accomplish two or three small goals.

In essence, *CEOs do this by thinking in what I call "action time-segments."* That is, "value" is expressed during each "work unit" of time. Yet it seems puzzling. How can it possibly inject value into time for executives to wander the hall and chat about projects large and small, as well as nonwork issues like sports and family? Yet here's the CEO time paradox—much of value does occur in these and myriad other casual encounters.

Let's table for the moment the rationale underlying this statement until the final section of this chapter, and begin by crystallizing three fundamental, time-based hallmarks that seem to underlie the "influencing" cast of mind.

Then will follow an outline of thirteen "influencing opportunities" to show you how you can start today to achieve multiple objectives by exerting influence on simultaneous fronts.

Three Hallmarks of CEO Time Management

1. Spotlight Thinking

CEOs practice an intense focus—if only for a minute or even seconds—on whatever they are doing. Until they have responded or made a decision, they don't let go. Throughout this book, this trait has surfaced in numerous different contexts, including instant TRAF, fast phone turnaround, and maintaining a steady course through days studded with myriads of interruptions. The flexible "ten-minute time segments" discussed in the context of an organized day (see page 111) are a result of spotlight thinking, as is the ascendance of "focused" tasking over multitasking.

These myriad punctuations of contact during the course of the day—both scheduled and unscheduled—offer what I call a "pop" of business. *CEOs ensure that each transaction—whether it's an interrup-*

*tion to answer a question, or a pause to return a call or respond to an
e-mail—becomes an opportunity to extend their sphere of influence.*
Think about the multiplier effect. If you were to have, say, ten opportunities to manage influence every day through "interruptions," that
adds up to 200 per month and 2,400 a year! Over the course of a career,
that can grow your influence in a company or industry exponentially.

Try this experiment: Begin practicing spotlight thinking as you
address your paperwork, return phone calls and e-mail, prepare
reports, or stop to answer a question, using all the relevant executive
organization and time-management tools described in those chapters. Instead of falling prey to the multitasking trend, try focusing
intently on the matter at hand until it is dealt with.

As you increase your ability to zoom in on things, you'll soon
find your decision-making muscle strengthening every day. This will
multiply your time to accomplish the critical tasks that grow your
influence in your own domain.

2. Ruthless Responsiveness

Take it from me: you will never, ever see a paperwork buildup on an
up-the-ladder CEO's desk. I may be a specialist in organization and
time management, but I'll confess that sometimes, owing to travel or
deadlines, paperwork can pile up on my desk for a couple of days, or
my in-box can become overextended. That is not the case with senior
executives. You will never see a two- or three-day buildup on the desk
of an up-the-ladder CEO. You will never see so much as an hour's
buildup. You will never see a ten-minute buildup. You will never see
any buildup of any description whatsoever!

For CEOs, there is no accumulation because there is nothing to
accumulate. The only way to describe this responsiveness is *ruthless.*

Of course, as these executives moved up the ladder, their assistants
vetted more materials for them. But you can count on the fact that,

brand manager or CEO, their reactions were the same: *Deal with it! Now.* This same attitude informs CEOs' ASAP turnaround response—whether personally or by someone else on their behalf—to phone calls and follow-ups.

It was amusing to see how top executives dropped their veil of formality when I brought up the subject of clean desks. They really talked like any of the rest of us in their intense response to this question of clean desks. Richard Snyder, past chairman of the book publisher Simon & Schuster, told me it drove him crazy to see papers remain on his desk for more than a day. He tolerated it only when circumstances made it impossible to conclude that item of business sooner.

As I have discovered, this ruthless responsiveness—ruthless in the sense that it seems to stem from an unyielding personal imperative—is another key tool supporting the executives' driving mission to manage influence. Here's a scenario that demonstrates how it works:

Luanne, the marketing director, drops a one-page summary report on the CEO's desk with this cover note:

Jack—FYI, this is an interesting summary of the Marketing
Council's findings re cross-industry marketing funds allocation
and their impact.

Luanne

At a minimum, I argue, the CEO will reply, perhaps by e-mail, with an acknowledgment and thanks. So the category of *ties and liens*—showing respect—is being addressed. And it's quite likely that, assuming the information is provocative, this CEO will ask Luanne to have her people analyze their company's marketing allocations into the same format as the Marketing Council's report, and distribute it for discussion at next month's marketing meeting. By doing that, the CEO is conveying several messages:

Appreciation for the information

Attitude conveyance: New ideas and approaches are welcome.

Nudge: Perhaps it's time to freshen up the marketing mix.

3. "Delegate 90 Percent of Everything That Crosses Your Desk"

"From the minute I walked in the door, I delegated 90 percent of everything that crossed my desk," said Hicks Waldron, former CEO of Avon. "It's the only way to succeed."

I'll warrant that virtually every executive who climbs to the top takes that advice to heart—for two reasons, one fairly direct, the other complex and deeply meaningful: first, delegation creates opportunities for the core project, managing influence; second, delegation releases and harnesses resources to "build an edifice."

DELEGATING TO CREATE OPPORTUNITIES FOR "MANAGING INFLUENCE"

This is a two-fold proposition: delegation releases time for managing influence, *and* delegating creates a primary platform through which managing influence can occur. If a CEO's primary task is to manage influence, then anything that distracts from that task is by definition to be reduced or eliminated. Thus, "delegating 90 percent of what crosses their desks" to release that time to manage influence more or less goes with the territory.

In addition, all the encounters required in the very process of delegation—discussing tasks, touching base, status updates, following up, etc.—in and of themselves provide a major platform, perhaps *the* major platform, for the manifold interactions of managing influence.

DELEGATING TO UNLEASH RESOURCES TO BUILD AN EDIFICE

In published interviews with up-the-ladder CEOs, one word that recurs constantly is "building": "building a business"; "building our credibility"; "building up our reserve"; "building a leadership network."

The materials executives use to build their businesses are the skills, energies, and drives of other people. Therefore, releasing, harnessing, and mobilizing those skills and energies through delegation—not only delegation of tasks, but delegation of broad responsibilities and goals—becomes a hallmark skill of successful executives at every level.

Said Larry Bossidy in his book *Execution,* "You can easily spot the doers by observing their work habits. They're the ones who energize people, are decisive on tough issues, *get things done through others* [my emphasis], and follow through as second nature."

How can you delegate more effectively?

1. *Have your priorities clearly in mind*—both task priorities and priority themes.

2. *Seek out tasks and opportunities to execute these priorities through others.*

3. *Formal reviews.* Talk things over in scheduled sit-downs at least every two weeks. Quarterly "big picture" reviews are also wise.

4. *Informal touch-bases,* or MBWA—"How ya doin'?" "Anything I can help you with?"—generous amounts of wide-open-door time to answer questions and troubleshoot. All of these are essential.

5. *Follow up, follow up, follow up* should be as natural as breathing.

Teodoro Benavides has given a lot of thought to how to make the "following up" process with staff work. He describes his strategy as follows: "I keep lists. I won't bug you every time. But they know I remember. Then every once in a while I'll ask, 'Do you remember that I asked you about this issue? And it's been about three weeks now.' I'm a high

**MATCHING PEOPLE WITH THEIR
STRENGTHS—INCLUDING YOUR OWN**

To be successful, an effective delegator must discover their employees' unique strengths instead of training them to conform.

Akio Morita, the founder of Sony, urged managers not to train new employees to fit the mold, but to study them, learn their strengths, and make the best use of their skills.

So, for instance, if one of your staff members has an attractive "hail fellow" quality, hand him or her assignments that take advantage of that trait.

As Morita observed in his autobiography, *Made in Japan,* an effective manager "has to combine [employees] in the best possible way, just as a master mason builds a stone wall. The stones are sometimes round, sometimes square . . . figure out how to put them together . . ."

Take a lead from Kent Crawford of PM Solutions, who took that approach to his *own* skills: "The biggest thing for me personally—strategy, visioning, and strategic direction—are the areas in which I am personally most effective, and in which my time is best spent. Then I build the buy-in among my executives, so they can translate that into actions and follow through."

Take time to think through your strong suits, and try to focus on them, and where possible, delegate to others those tasks that call for a different strength.

'entrust' kind of guy. And I'll not let it go. What you don't want me to do is to be in your business. If I'm in your business, you're in trouble."

Benavides types his delegation lists into his computer, noting the person, the project, when he gave it to the person, and when it was done. He said, "I pull those lists out at the end of the year, and it has a lot to do with my staff's performance reviews."

He meets with his top staff individually for an hour every two weeks, and he might take out the list—without waiting until the end of the year. He might say, "Wow, I'm impressed that you took care of that task so quickly," or "You know, that project just took too long." He'll also keep an eye on workload, being careful not to overuse the most eager staffers who keep saying, "Give me more!" Sometimes he will shift projects around, or extend due dates if possible, if he feels someone is overloaded.

Bossidy makes the important point that this kind of attentive delegating has nothing to do with micromanaging. Micromanaging is interfering at an inappropriate level of detail with the means and tactics your direct reports use to accomplish their tasks.

Attentive delegation has more to do with navigating: Are we moving in the right direction? Are there shoals and rapids that need to be negotiated? What problems are emerging, and how can we engage with them and solve them? What opportunities are available for development?

So, at the top executive levels, delegating 90 percent of what comes across your desk doesn't mean getting rid of it. In a sense, it means becoming a gardener—articulating, shepherding, managing, navigating, releasing the skills, energies, and leadership abilities of others toward common goals.

A Delegation Audit

Before deciding to retain a task for yourself, ask yourself whether or not it should be reassigned. Delegate the following tasks:

- Tasks unrelated to your personal strengths.
- Tasks no longer commensurate with your present level.
- Tasks that do not correspond to your high-payoff components.

- Tasks that a more junior person can do or can be trained to do.
- Tasks that fit into another's specialty, whether an in-house person or an outside consultant.

Tip: Identify repetitive tasks (requests for materials, information, prices, etc.) that can be permanently assigned elsewhere.

Also, we forget that parts of a task can often be reassigned or shared:

- *Draft:* Give key ideas to someone else who will draft the report.
- *Edit/revise:* Sketch out a rough report, memo, or brochure for another to edit, revise, or polish.
- *Summarize:* Ask staffers to summarize long reports and flag materials for your attention.
- *Prepare recommendations:* Staffers should present proposals and problems to you, with their solutions and recommendations.
- *Do research; gather background information:* Gather backup data such as statistics, documentation, and history. For example, a lawyer reviving an old case asked paralegals to list previously filed materials so he could pinpoint what he needed without personally going through the files.

How to Delegate When You Don't Have Anyone to Delegate To

Don't yet have that staff to delegate 90 percent of your tasks to? Turn to the next best thing: Delegate onerous or timewasting tasks to the dustbin of history—by eliminating them; by teaming up with others; or by "checkerboarding" tasks to suit people's strengths.

Old habits die hard. So, to put this analysis in motion, list over the course of an average week or so all your tasks, ranging from basic TRAF to the most complex report or spreadsheet. Then work through your list as follows:

Eliminate. Are there tasks you regularly perform that would leave the world no worse off if they were eliminated—perhaps the third proofreading of a document, or a report you prepare that no one uses? If you have a discretionary choice, then just stop doing the task and monitor the results for a week or so. If no one notices, then it's over.

When you don't feel you can eliminate a task on your own, try making a case to your manager. One marketing manager went in to his boss and said, "Rob, I was wondering whether you thought preparing the such-and-such report every week is the most productive use of my time? Do you consult it? You've never actually asked me about it, and neither has anyone else."

Sure enough, Rob agreed that that report had just become part of the wallpaper, and it was eliminated.

Team up. On page 163, I described how a specialist in Far Eastern currency fluctuation, in preparing a report, consulted a colleague with special know-how about Asia. This is "teaming up." There are many legitimate opportunities to consult with colleagues to make a project fuller and richer. And because working with others collegially is often more satisfying, it mobilizes your energies, thereby increasing your efficiency.

"Checkerboard." And then there are the must-do tasks that you find dull, onerous, or stressful. Or maybe you just don't do them well. Guess what. Somewhere in this world there is someone for whom the task you detest is enjoyable child's play. And that person may be sitting at the next desk.

Think of a checkerboard of skills—your own and your colleagues'—with the object being to move tasks from where they are performed less skillfully and enjoyably to where they are performed more so.

For example, Ellen, a retailing executive who hated basic TRAF and was always behind in her paperwork and e-mails, asked a colleague, Sam, to review her incoming materials each day just to make sure that while she was away on a buying trip to the Far East, something didn't come up that she needed to know about. To Sam, this was nothing, so when she returned, rather than facing the stacks she was dreading, there were a few items Sam felt she should look at personally, and a list of people to whom he had distributed various items.

What a guy! Ellen immediately asked Sam if he could become her "chief of staff" in exchange for an onerous task that she could do for him—and it worked.

What's the time-management benefit here, since no tasks were eliminated, and time was still being put in? This is Organizing Law No. 9:

ORGANIZING LAW NO. 9:
Heighten productivity by seeking out projects
that engage your interest and energy.

MANAGING YOUR BOSS

Keeping your manager always informed, and acknowledging his or her personal way of doing things, is the other side of the coin of successful delegation. Ted Benavides's advice to managers at every level is "I would always find time to keep your bosses informed of what's going on, because they hate surprises. And then you need to find what the best way is to get that information to them."

For example, Benavides described how he personally likes his folks to send him an e-mail, bulleting in advance the main points they want to discuss. "If your boss is this kind of a person, give him or her advance notice. Whereas another kind of boss will just consider an advance e-mail to be an annoyance and getting in the way."

One managing editor tells the story of how she constantly e-mailed her publisher with queries or notes, but received no

(cont'd on page 226)

MANAGING YOUR BOSS *(cont'd from page 225)*

response, whereas when she left a phone message, her publisher always called her back promptly. Finally she asked her boss, "Do you prefer the phone to e-mails?" The reply was, "Oh yes!" It was almost as if the publisher hadn't articulated that preference to herself until she was asked.

So it's always worthwhile to try to evaluate your supervisor's preferred modes of operation.

Trading Up: Along the Arc of Executive Possibility

Thirteen Influencing Opportunities

If you begin to incorporate the three primary hallmarks of CEO time management—spotlight thinking; instant responsiveness to all documents, calls, etc; and intense delegation combined with relentless tracking and follow-up—you will find new opportunities to manage influence within your own sphere at work every day.

If you have a pet project, mention it often, casually. In every encounter, no matter how slight, if you consciously act on at least two of the thirteen options described below, you will greatly expand your influence and multiply your productivity—like a CEO.

Seek out opportunities to expand your connections with others. For instance, one marketing director, as mentioned before, makes it her business to hand-carry materials to the publicity department so she can easily touch base with at least three or four people along the way. Katharine Graham, when she went down to the newsroom to visit the editor, took the opportunity to touch base with at least five or six people along the way. "If one person is busy," she said, "that gives me the opportunity to say hello to someone I haven't spoken with for a while."

Another easy, informal way to stay in touch with all your colleagues is to take a different route every time you move around the building. You will multiply your opportunities for casual hallway conversation. Remember, don't try to push or force anything. You're not trying to manipulate people. You're just adding in a little of your own energy. Mostly, such encounters are glancing. It's the accumulated impact that can be so powerful.

And now, in this final section of the book, to give you a boost up on the process of learning how to manage influence, I'll describe some practical examples of how to achieve a multiplier influencing effect in various aspects of your everyday work.

The interactions I suggest here fall into thirteen categories—several of which were developed by Andrew S. Grove in his book *High Output Management;* others I created based on my intensive study of CEOs.

Taken together, they offer endless opportunities for managing influence. If a hundred or more brief nudges occur over the course of a week, and thousands over months and years—then you've set a powerful force in motion, a process of influencing others that will, over time, leverage massive effects—all the way to the top.

THIRTEEN INFLUENCING OPPORTUNITIES

Opportunities for Influence	Comments
Strengthen ties and liens.	The head of a large company personally calls a fellow CEO to request a copy of a report. The request is not significant, but the contact is. Keeping the network of contacts in good repair could be called a *(cont'd on page 228)*

(cont'd from page 227)

Opportunities for Influence	Comments
	"shadow priority"—a situation where the contact *itself* is the priority, independent of the content of the call or drop-in.

To adapt this key agenda: Call someone, internal or external, whose connection you consider valuable. Request a report or solicit their advice on a particular topic. You'll strengthen your rapport, regardless of your actual need for the report or advice. |
| Receive and give information. | Jon Hanson, head of The Hampshire Companies, a New Jersey real estate invest-ment firm, says, "If once a month I were to just take five minutes of my time [to inquire about customer service and problem solv-ing], it gives me . . . a little pulse . . . as to what goes on."

Barbara Ley Toffler said, discussing her book *Final Accounting,* which describes the collapse of Arthur Andersen, "One of the most important things for every leader to recognize is the saying, 'Know what you should know.' Leaders of organizations should make every effort to get all the information, even if they don't want to hear it."

To adapt this key agenda: Schedule a reminder on your calendar each month to spend five minutes checking in with a critical peer—say in IT—just to find out what's happening in their arena. You may pick up trends or just establish a connection that could be immensely helpful if you get |

Opportunities for Influence	Comments
	into a crunch. In general, as Toffler said, "Know what you should know."
Emphasize developing ideas as distinct from originating them.	In his autobiography, Lee Iacocca said, "The best way to develop ideas is through interacting with your fellow managers . . . simply shooting the breeze, helping each other out, and solving problems." An executive mandate is less to originate ideas than to establish an environment in which discussions can flourish, and to guide team members so their creative energies are productively focused. *To adapt this key agenda:* Suggest regular informal "brainstorming" get-togethers with your peers, just to toss around big ideas you never seem to have time to discuss. Get the creative ball rolling by tossing out an idea of your own.
Articulate a vision.	The genius of a great executive is to articulate a vision by eliciting and melding together the full range of ideas and contributions from his or her team. *To adapt this key agenda:* If your department doesn't have a mission statement, talk with your colleagues on a casual basis about their sense of your department's mission. Perhaps volunteer to help draw one together with input from your colleagues. Management will have a clearer focus of what your department sees as its vision within the company, which will help everyone define their goals more clearly. *(cont'd on page 230)*

(cont'd from page 229)

Opportunities for Influence	Comments
Lobby and be lobbied.	John Reed, when he was at Citicorp, remarked, "I am lobbied. People try to capture me and push me in a given direction, and that's part of my job, to be available for that. And my mind gets changed."
	To adapt this key agenda: If you have an idea you think is worth exploring, lobby your colleagues (gently and humorously) and your boss to make your case. Conversely, encourage staff to lobby you—make their case—with fresh ideas.
Do reconnaissance—pick up potential problems and rumblings.	A Citicorp executive, speaking of retired Citicorp CEO Walter Wriston's subtle style of reconnaissance, said that he always had "a wary ear open to be alert to situations . . . that might not surface in the ordinary routine of the management information flows . . . He picks up a sense of dissent or difference of opinion and works it into his total appraisal."
	To adapt this key agenda: During the general course of meetings or informal chats around the water cooler, keep your ear to the ground. If your gut instinct tells you that something is amiss, or out of the normal run, listen carefully to what you're hearing so you can absorb the context of it into your own work or decisions.
Nudge.	There are many small things a manager can do to influence an associate: make a phone call suggesting a particular approach to a decision; send a note outlining one's own view of a particular

Opportunities for Influence	Comments
	situation; make a comment during a meeting. Says Andrew Grove in *High Output Management:*
	In such instances you may be advocating a preferred course of action, but you are not issuing an instruction or command. Yet, you are doing something stronger than merely conveying information.
	Let's call it "nudging" because through it you nudge an individual or a meeting in the direction you would like. This is an immensely important managerial activity. For every unambiguous decision we make, we probably nudge things a dozen times . . .
	I can also influence groups not under my direct supervision by making observations to those who manage them.
	To adapt this key agenda: If you have a project going nowhere, try "nudging" the key players by sending an article showing how another company implemented this concept successfully. Or, when someone does take a positive step, e-mail them with an encouraging note, and copy everyone else, which conveys the message that their efforts are appreciated and will be rewarded.
Act as a role model.	"Values and behavioral norms . . . are conveyed very effectively by doing and doing *visibly.*" Thus a manager's sharing of information and authority, fairness, decision-making style, ethics, all have an impact on immediate *(cont'd on page 232)*

(cont'd from page 231)

Opportunities for Influence	Comments
	subordinates in modeling their own styles, and so down through the organization. *To adapt this key agenda:* If ethical behavior in your company has been an issue of late, demonstrate your own ethical commitment by showing that your word is your bond in all dealings with staff, colleagues, and customers.
Offer personal support. Strengthen ties.	Give a sincere compliment. Strengthen ties through a bit of banter or personal chat. *To adapt this key agenda:* Take a few minutes each week and ask people what they're planning for that weekend or vacation, which shows interest in them as human beings.
Suggest a correction in course, or even reprimand.	If something isn't bearing fruit, offer, "Why don't you try . . . ?" or "You know, over at International Widget they had good results with . . ." or even, "You let the team down, Joe, on this one." *To adapt this key agenda:* If someone on your project team is having problems accomplishing his or her end of the task, offer to listen and make a suggestion on another resource they might turn to for help.
Facilitate, troubleshoot, monitor deadlines.	Ask, "What's new with that project? Anything you could use from me?" *To adapt this key agenda:* Find the balance between driving people crazy by over-pressing and being a supportive and continuous presence.

Opportunities for Influence	Comments
Move actions foward.	John Kotter, in his book *The General Managers*, when referring to a young executive on the rise, said she was aware of the need to make linkages—"knowing what needed to be done and who you had to work through to get it done."
	To adapt this key agenda: First ask yourself, "What needs to be done to move this project forward?" For example, you may need to gain a buy-in from people who aren't natural allies. Then ask, "Who do I need to work through to get it done?" Smooth the way by consulting in advance with one person in the group who is a center of influence.
Demand feedback.	A study of failed CEOs by consultant Ram Charan indicated that a key trait of successful executives was the emotional strength to demand honest and candid feedback about the performance of key subordinates—and about oneself.
	One executive who famously requested active feedback was former New York City mayor Edward I. Koch, who asked constantly, "How'm I doing?"
	To adapt this key agenda: If your firm doesn't have peer review, suggest it as a means of getting honest feedback on how you—and everyone else—are really doing. Or hold a postmortem on a project with the team members, giving people a chance to comment obliquely on what—and who—made the effort a success or failure.

The net result of this unique way of managing influence is a highly distinctive time-management strategy that is characterized by exchanging many, many brief connections over the day—each one an opportunity to influence and be influenced. These connections are a primary reason successful executives are able to "multiply" time and reach exponential levels of accomplishment.

The good news is that the concept of managing influence is applicable to you, no matter where you are on the corporate ladder. Even if these CEO time-management behaviors don't come instinctively, you have the option of modifying or adapting them—as well as any or all organization and time-management strategies explained throughout this book.

By utilizing these strategies, you can act as a CEO in your own domain. You can operate with the same efficiency as top executives and build your sphere of influence.

Even if you're not aiming for the boardroom, you will maximize and leverage your productivity by trying some of these techniques. If nothing else, you'll experience the magic of "multiplying time." And who doesn't wish for more hours in the day?

The 9 Organizing Laws

1. Relentlessly process all papers and e-mails, personally or through an assistant.

2. Make decisions, even if they need to be revised later.

3. Foolproof follow-up is a linchpin of organization.

4. Never use e-mail when a verbal discussion is more efficient.

5. Return all phone calls within 24 hours—personally or through a staffer.

6. Gain power and productivity by managing, rather than trying to control, the changeability of the day.

7. Claim an hour of priority time every day.

8. Seed your routine tasks throughout the day, rather than trying to carve out blocks of time.

9. Heighten productivity by seeking out projects that engage your interest and energy.

Selected Bibliography

Books and Articles

Allen, David. *Work Smarter Not Harder: Roadmap to Success.* A *Fast Company* Publication, 1998.

———. *Getting Things Done: The Art of Stress-Free Productivity.* New York: Viking, 2001.

Baldoni, John. *Personal Leadership: Taking Control of Your Worklife.* Rochester, MI: Elsewhere Press, 2001.

Beardsley, David. "Don't Manage Time, Manage Yourself." *Fast Company,* April/May 1998.

Bodow, Steve. "Microsofter." *The New York Times Magazine,* November 24, 2002.

Bossidy, Larry and Charan, Ram. *Execution: The Discipline of Getting Things Done.* New York: Crown Business, 2002.

Botkin, James W. *Smart Business: How Knowledge Communities Can Revolutionize Your Company.* New York: Free Press, 1999.

Calonius, Erik. "How Top Managers Manage Their Time." *Fortune,* June 4, 1990.

Chadderdon, Lisa. "Merrill Lynch Works—At Home." *Fast Company,* April/May 1998.

Charan, Ram and Colvin, Geoffrey. "Why CEOs Fail." *Fortune,* June 21, 1999.

Ciancutti, Arky and Steding, Thomas L. *Built on Trust.* New York: Contemporary Publishing, 2000.

Collins, Eliza G. C., Editor. *Executive Success: Making It in Management* (a collection of articles from the Harvard Business Review). New York: John Wiley & Sons, Inc., 1983.

Collins, Jim. *Good to Great: Why Some Companies Make the Leap . . . and Others Don't.* New York: HarperBusiness, 2001.

Cooper, Kenneth. *Regaining the Power of Youth at Any Age.* Nashville, TN: Thomas Nelson Publishers, 1999.

Covey, Stephen R. *The Seven Habits of Highly Effective People.* New York: Free Press, 1989.

Deutschman, Alan. "The CEO's Secret of Managing Time." *Fortune,* June 1, 1992.

Drucker, Peter F. *The Effective Executive.* New York: HarperBusiness, 1993.

Erdman, Andrew. "Secrets of Great Second Bananas." *Fortune,* May 6, 1991.

Field, Anne. "Attention Deficit Is in the Office, Too." *The New York Times,* September 22, 2002.

Fox, Jeffrey J. *How to Become CEO: The Rules for Rising to the Top of Any Organization.* New York: Hyperion Books, 1998.

Gates, Bill. *Business @ the Speed of Thought.* New York: Warner Books, 2000.

Goldsmith, Marshall and Belasco, James, Eds. *Leading Authorities on Business.* Washington, D.C.: Leading Authorities, 2002.

Grove, Andrew. *High Output Management.* New York: Random House, 1983.

Hannon, Kerry. "Beat the Time Church—and Take a Vacation." *YourCompany—Forecast 1997.*

Harvard Business Review. *Interviews with CEOs.* Boston: Harvard Business School Press, 2000.

Helgesen, Sally. *The Web of Inclusion.* New York: Currency/Doubleday, 1995.

Hymowitz, Carol. "In the Lead." *The Wall Street Journal,* December 29, 1998.

Iacocca, Lee and Novak, William. *Iacocca.* New York: Bantam Books, 1999.

Johnson, Spencer, *The Present.* New York: Doubleday, 2003.

Kahaner, Larry. *Competitive Intelligence.* New York: Touchstone/Simon & Schuster, 1998.

Kaye, Steve. *The Manager's Pocket Guide to Effective Meetings.* Amherst, MA: HRD Press, 1999.

Kocar, Joy Soto. "Managing Time with Database." *The HP Palmtop Paper.* www.palmtoppaper.com, September/October 1996.

Kotter, John P. *The General Managers.* New York: The Free Press, 1982.

Kriegel, Robert J. *How to Succeed in Business Without Working So Damn Hard.* New York: Warner Business Books, 2002.

Lakein, Alan. *How to Get Control of Your Time and Your Life.* New York: Crown Publishing Group, 1980.

Lamott, Anne. *Bird by Bird.* New York: Random House, 1994.

Latour, Almar. "Electrolux CEO Fits Future in the Palm of His Hand." *The Wall Street Journal,* June 18, 1999.

Mackenzie, Alec. *The Time Trap: How to Get More Done in Less Time* (rev. ed.). New York: AMACOM, 1999.

Mintzberg, Henry. *The Nature of Managerial Work.* New York: Harper & Row, 1973.

Morita, Akio. *Made in Japan: Akio Morita & Sony.* New York: E. P. Dutton, 1986.

Nilson, Carolyn. *More Team Games for Trainers.* New York: McGraw-Hill, 1997.

Noble, Sara F., ed. *301 Great Management Ideas from America's Most Innovative Small Companies.* Boston: Inc. Publications, 1995.

Ong, Laureen with Abby Ellin. "Purposeful Exploration." *The New York Times.* April 27, 2003.

Overholt, Alison. "The Art of Multitasking." *Fast Company.* October, 2002.

Peters, Tom. *The Circle of Innovation.* New York: Knopf, 1997.

Pickering, Peg. *How to Make the Most of Your Workday.* Franklin Lakes, NJ: The Career Press, 2001.

Rogers, George D. Article on John D. Rockefeller. *Saturday Evening Post,* July 30, 1921.

Schwab, Charles R. *Charles Schwab's Guide to Financial Independence.* New York: Three Rivers Press, 1998.

Stein, Murray S. and Walker, John R. *Triumph over Shyness.* New York: McGraw-Hill, 2001.

Stewart, Martha (verbatim interview). "At the Desk of Martha Stewart." *Business 2.0,* June 2002.

Sutton, Gary. *The Six-Month Fix: Adventures in Rescuing Failing Companies.* New York: John Wiley & Sons, 2001.

Toffler, Barbara Ley. *Final Accounting: Ambition, Greed, and the Fall of Arthur Andersen.* New York: Broadway, 2003.

Welch, Jack with Byrne, John A. *Jack: Straight from the Gut.* New York: Warner Books, 2001.

White, Shira P. *New Ideas about New Ideas.* Cambridge: Perseus Books, 2002.

Winston, Stephanie. *The Organized Executive.* New York: Warner Books, 2001.

Worthy, Ford S. "How CEOs Manage Their Time." *Fortune,* January 18, 1988.

no author cited. "Style, and Substance." *Forbes,* June 15, 1987.

no author cited. "How Early Do You Have to Get Up to Swim with the Sharks?" *The New York Times,* July 13, 1997.

Periodicals

The Baltimore Sun; Book Marketing Update; The Boston Globe; Bottom Line/ Personal; Business Week; CIO [Chief Information Officer] *Magazine; Communication Briefings* (newsletter); www.darwinmag.com; *Fast Company; Inc.; The New York Times; The Organized Executive* (newsletter); *Personal Excellence* (newsletter); *The Wall Street Journal*

Participating Executives

The executives listed here were kind enough to offer me their time and insights into executive organization and time management, which were distilled into *Organized for Success.* Many thanks for their generosity and attentive concern to render their experience into a framework that could be useful to others.

Larry Alterwitz. CEO, Walker Furniture Company, Las Vegas, NV.

Mary Rudie Barneby. UBS Warburg, New York, NY.

Dennis Bass. Deputy Directory, Center for Science in the Public Interest, Washington, DC.

Teodoro J. Benavides. City Manager, City of Dallas, Dallas, TX.

William J. Bratton. Chief of Police, Los Angeles Police Department, Los Angeles, CA.

Gaston Caperton. President, College Board, New York, NY. Formerly Governor of West Virginia.

Akira Chiba. President, Pokémon USA, Inc., New York, NY.

Terry Conrad. CEO, Merz Pharmaceuticals USA, Greensboro, NC.

Luke Corbett. Chairman & CEO, The Kerr-McGee Company, Oklahoma City, OK.

J. Kent Crawford. CEO, PM Solutions (a project management consulting, training, and research firm), Havertown, PA.

John Curley. Chairman & CEO (ret.), Gannett, Arlington, VA.

Faye Davis. Vice-President, Sprint—Enterprise Property Services, Overland Park, KS.

William G. Dugan. Publisher, Briefings Publishing Group, Alexandria, VA.

Martin Edelston. President & Founder, Boardroom Inc., Stamford, CT.

Jenette E. Fetzner. VP/National Accounts, CIGNA, Hartford, CT.

Julie Flagg (Dr.). Managing physician of multiple-physician practice, Wesleyan, CT.

Jack Gallaway. President & Chief Operating Officer (ret.), Isle of Capri Casinos, Biloxi, MS.

Verna Gibson. Past President & CEO, The Limited Stores, Columbus, OH.

Robert J. Giordano. President & CEO, MRB Investor Relations, New York, NY.

Ronald Goldsberry. Chairman, OnStation Corporation (a provider of Internet-based channel-enabling technology), San Mateo, CA.

Katharine Graham. Chairman (dec.), The Washington Post Companies, Washington, DC.

Carol Gregor. AVP/National Accounts, CIGNA, Hartford, CT.

Jon Hanson, Chairman, Hampshire Companies (a real estate investment firm), Morristown, NJ. Formerly headed the Meadowlands by appointment of former NJ Governor Thomas Kean.

Idit Harel. CEO, MaMaMedia (a "new media" interactive website for children and families), New York, NY.

Robert Hemenway. Chancellor, The University of Kansas, Lawrence, KS.

Karen Horn. Managing Director, Marsh Private Client Services (a subsidiary of Marsh & McLennan), New York, NY.

Sandra Kresch. Independent consultant specializing in strategic change. Formerly a partner at Booz Allen & Hamilton, New York, NY.

Brian Kurtz. Executive Vice President, Boardroom Inc., Stamford, CT.

Nancy L. Lane. VP/Community Relations (ret.), Johnson & Johnson, New Brunswick, NJ.

Leonard A. Lauder. Chairman, The Estée Lauder Companies, Inc., New York, NY.

Arthur Levitt. Chairman of the Securities and Exchange Commission in the Clinton administration.

John Tepper Marlin. Chief Economist/Office of Comptroller, City of New York, New York, NY.

James M. Morris II. Chairman and CEO, Signator Financial Network (an affiliate of John Hancock Life Insurance Company), Boston, MA.

Karen A. Page. Chair, Harvard Business School Network of Women Alumnae.

George Pickett (Dr.). Medical Director of the West Virginia Institute of Medicine. Former President of the American Public Health Association.

Leeanne Probst-Engels. AVP/National Accounts, CIGNA, Hartford, CT.

Gerard R. Roche. Senior Chairman, Heidrick & Struggles, Inc., New York, NY.

Richard Snyder. Former Chairman & CEO, Simon & Schuster, New York, NY.

Peter Vandevanter. Vice President, New Venture Division, Knight-Ridder, Charlotte, NC.

Joseph Vittoria. Chairman, ResortQuest International, Inc. (a vacation rental property management company), Destin, FL. Formerly Chairman & CEO, Avis, Inc., Garden City, NY.

Jeanette Sarkisian Wagner. Vice Chairman (ret.), The Estée Lauder Companies Inc., New York, NY.

Hicks Waldron. Chairman & CEO (ret.), Avon Corporation, New York, NY.

Marcia Zerivitz. Executive Director & Founder, Jewish Museum of Florida, Miami, FL.

Index